SPACE
Marketing

Competing in the new commercial space industry

By Izzy House

Special thanks to:

Jim – My dear husband that supported my journey.

Dee - My sister for being proud of this space nerd.

Chelsea – My book-writing buddy who encouraged me.

Paul - My Space Uncle who encouraged me to reach for the stars!

To my Civil Air Patrol family that ignited my passion for aerospace and the cadets who inspired me to go for my dreams of space.

... and all of my friends and colleagues for your support!

CONTENTS

Foreword to Space Marketing

When John F. Kennedy announced his goal of becoming the first nation to place a man on the Moon before the end of the 1960s, nobody knew how such a daunting project could be achieved in such a short period of time. What everyone did know is that the Apollo program would cost money. A huge amount of money. In fact, between the years 1963 and 1969, the United States of America spent an average of 3.3% of the federal budget on NASA; from 1965 to 1968, it surpassed 4%.

How did NASA and Kennedy convince the American public to fund such an audacious plan?

Marketing.

"The astronauts became the leading edge of one of the biggest marketing efforts in history," Captain Eugene A. Cernan told me about ten years ago. Flying to the Moon not once, but twice on Apollo 10 and Apollo 17, Cernan also holds the distinction of being the second American to walk in space and the last man to have left his footprints on the lunar surface. "Along the way, and totally unexpected by us, we astronauts became very visible public figures. This wasn't NASA's initial intent, but they adapted quickly. It was the press, and in turn the public, who declared us 'heroes,' and from that followed the inevitable responsibility to 'market' the space program, both to Congress and to the public that elected it. We were the voices of a nation marketing the United States of America."

Cernan and his fellow astronauts became the public face of the 400,000 people from the government, industry, media, and academics who worked on Apollo. Leading the marketing charge were the professional journalists and marketers who worked within the NASA Public Affairs Office. Working closely with hundreds of public relations professionals from contractors including Raytheon, Boeing, Grumman, and IBM who built parts of the Apollo spacecraft and associated materials, NASA Public Affairs operated like a newsroom to rapidly disseminate information to the world press.

Unlike the secretive Russian space program which only announced missions once they had succeeded, NASA ran an open program. NASA Public Affairs chief during the Apollo project, Julian Scheer, argued passionately for making real-time audio and video of the missions public, as well as outfitting the spacecraft with high quality cameras and teaching the astronauts how to use them. His efforts at getting the word out to the American public and to the citizens of the world was as important to the success of the Apollo program as anybody's in the program including that of the first man to walk on the Moon.

More than 50 years later, were in the middle of a new space race. This time, its private companies competing. Some of the strategies to generate attention are the same today as they were in the days of black and white television. This time, the people capturing the public's imagination aren't government employees—the astronauts who risked their lives to travel to the moon. Instead, they are tech billionaires including Jeff Bezos, Richard Branson, and Elon Musk who are risking part of their vast fortunes to build spacecraft for paying customers.

Like the astronauts of the 1960s, the public is fascinated with the exploits of the new space pioneers and they're feeding the public's interest through the media and directly by holding launch events, selling merchandise, and creating amazing content including live and recorded video.

However, there's a lot that's new. Imagine Neil Armstrong sharing his famous words: "That's one small step for [a] man, one giant leap for mankind" on social media! Today, generating attention is as easy as a tweet for people like Musk (@elonmusk with 58 million followers), Branson (@richardbranson with 12 million followers), and their companies including SpaceX with 17 million Twitter followers.

Social media means instant and free communications and has been embraced by the new players as well as NASA, with 47 million Twitter followers.

These new ideas for how to generate attention may seem bothersome for companies that just want to get on with building sophisticated technologies, but as Izzy House says in these pages: "A company may have the best idea, but it takes marketing for the world to see it."

Izzy shares proven marketing strategies and tactics including branding, social media, search engine optimization, and content generation. She shows you how to build relationships with existing and potential customers rather than just selling to them.

You will learn how to use modern versions of the kinds of marketing that put humans on the surface of the Moon. Izzy updates the idea of content as a marketing asset to be much more than what NASA public affairs and the contractors during the Apollo program delivered, the live television, stunning photographs, and well-written reports that were devoured by the news media and the public. Now content includes creating for YouTube, Instagram, TikTok, blogs, and much more.

It's still about educating and informing instead of interrupting and selling, but now there are new ways to market space.

Now it's your turn. Here's to your success,

David Meerman Scott
Business growth strategist and *Wall Street Journal* bestselling author of twelve books including *Marketing the Moon*
www.DavidMeermanScott.com
@dmscott

INTRODUCTION

ABOUT THE AUTHOR

Marketing expert and space nerd. Yep-that's me.

When I was 13, I spent the summer with my grandparents in Melbourne, Florida. This visit echoed through my life.

They were space shuttle crazy! They could see the launches from their back yard. Memorabilia peppered their home. Artwork depicting the program adorned the walls and a set of shuttle lamps were next to their bed. My grandfather even wore a gold shuttle pendent that the cargo bay doors opened to reveal a diamond. They had space fever bad!

Instead of a trip to Disney World, I got to go to Kennedy Space Center. My young self was a little disappointed when I was informed of this news. However, it turned out to be an amazing experience that would influence decades of my life.

During this summer trip, they also exposed me to science fiction books. I returned to the school year eager to be a biologist that would be selected for colonization to another planet.

It was here that peer pressure got to me. As I talked about my aspirations, I got that look. You know the one... the shocked, questioning look that suggested I might be out of my mind. If you are reading this book, you probably know it all too well.

As a result, my ambitions were grounded, and I sought another career. I landed on marketing. I got my degree and was cutting edge in my marketing knowledge until suddenly... I wasn't., marketing has drastically changed within the past ten years. This shift didn't sit well with me.

I found myself at a crossroads. My son had just graduated high school and I began thinking about what chapter three would look like in my book of life. I decided to return to school.

I am glad I did. It fed my mind and inspired me. I attained Valedictorian for a Bachelors in Internet Marketing. I was top student for the Bachelor's program and for the Masters in Digital Marketing program.

I loved working with small businesses during my career but felt that I needed to change things up. But what did that look like?

I got my answer in the summer of 2018. Standing in front of the space shuttle Atlantis, with tears in my eyes and my heart ready to burst, I realized that I could combine both of my passions. I returned to the school year eager to market space.

I still get those looks but I am no longer a 13-year-old that is swayed by them. In fact, now I convert those looks to ones of understanding, curiosity, and inspiration. I am a marketing expert after all. ☺

Booklist

Below are some recommended books that I have found to be influential in my point of view and that you may find useful in your space marketing journey.

One author, in particular, has been a huge part of my marketing DNA. David Meerman Scott has molded a large part of my marketing point-of-view. It would be difficult to pinpoint one area, kind of like trying to separate the oxygen molecule from the atmosphere. He authored many of the books that served as my textbooks while attending university and provided a strong foundation for my education. His research in *Marketing the Moon* help define my choice to pursue marketing in the space industry. He has been very instrumental in my career. Thank you!

Recommended marketing books:
Marketing the Moon by David Meerman Scott and Richard Jurek
Fanocracy by David Meerman Scott and Reiko Scott
Killing Marketing by Joe Pulizzi and Robert Rose
Epic Content Marketing by Joe Pulizzi
Stories that Stick by Kindra Hall
Great by Choice and *Good to Great* by Jim Collins and Morten T. Hansen
Marketing Rebellion: The Most Human Company Wins by Mark Schaefer
Building a StoryBrand: Clarify Your Message So Customers Will Listen by Donald Miller
Winfluence by Jason Falls
They Ask You Answer by Marcus Sheridan
Measure What Matters by John Doerr

WHY THIS BOOK

How can you change the world if no one knows you exist?
Marketing is about making your ideas, products, and services known. Call it outreach, public affairs, conversation, or promotion - these are all facets of marketing.

Two Reasons for this book:
1. Promote space.
   - Create awareness of our vital connection to space.
   - Generate excitement and spur education.
2. Help space companies thrive.
   - Adapt to the changing business model for the space industry.
   - Promote the understanding of marketing strategies and tactics through the lens of space.

Let's unpack these reasons.

1. Promoting space

Marketing is the tool that promotes anything, including space. The more entities that are involved in the process, the better the space industry will do as a whole. If space is not marketed, or promoted, then growth of the industry will be stunted.

There are too many things that come from space to leave this vital connection to chance. Everyone involved must do their part to grow the industry to reach its vibrant potential.

Everyone will benefit from the things that will result from our reaching the stars.

For example, as we travel to other moons and planets, we will need to develop new fuels to get us there. Last time I checked, there were no dinosaurs beyond Earth. However, water is located everywhere. Hydrogen rocket fuel is one of the fuels that will be developed to make this journey. How does this technology effect our cars, trucks, boats, factories, and other fuel-consuming processes here on Earth? How will this new fuel effect pollution? It could change our world for the better.

We need to let the world know. This is marketing.

Create awareness of our vital connection to space

How many people think about space and understand what is occurring right above our heads? The quote "out of sight, out of mind" is a major concern for the relationship between the public and their reliance on space. People make decisions about the future of space when they vote, support an idea or ideology, or buy a product. If space concerns are not top-of-mind, it will not have the support it needs to thrive.

Space needs to be marketed unless we want the next 50 years to be like the last. (...and that would be a very bad thing!)

Many people do not perceive the connection between their lives and space.
As taxes rise and conversations go back to the cost of NASA's endeavors, the public begins to question the need for exploration when "there are things that need to be done here on Earth." People are ignorant of how space enters into their lives. Some things may seem obvious like satellites providing services for our internet and phones, but the public may not connect these modern conveniences to the results of space exploration. Marketing through education can eliminate this ignorance.

When was the last time you heard someone say on the phone, "Hey, this is pretty amazing! I can't believe that my voice is going up to space and back down to you!" Nope. They're not saying that or even thinking it. It has become so common that it doesn't even enter into thought.

It is important to note that while the goal of reaching the Moon, Mars, and asteroids have their own level of importance, *it is the discoveries along the journey that brings about change here on Earth and creates the biggest changes in our everyday lives.*

The general population needs to be reminded of this personal and intimate connection that they have with space research. That conversation happens through marketing.

Generate excitement and spur educational initiatives.

Education is a form of marketing. It is the most important form of all of them in my opinion. We are selling the idea of space exploration and selling a career choice. It should be approached with a sense of humility, reverence, and obligation because someone will be dedicating their life's work to the cause.

More students need to participate in Science, Technology, Engineering, and Math (STEM) programs. STEAM programs add an A for the Arts component. Creativity is a necessary skill for solving the complex problems involved with leaving the planet and living beyond the atmosphere.

The education system in the U.S. has a tight structure of requirements that revolve around specific testing program for students. It tends to hog the stage and can push STEM/STEAM programs out of the curriculum. STEM/STEAM will only become a priority in schools if it is demanded by the public, the faculty, and the students.

Schools face many challenges that consume their focus. One of these challenges is the engagement of their students. I have personally witnessed aerospace classes being replaced with hip-hop classes in an effort to engage these students. Marketing initiatives have the power to get students excited about STEM/STEAM careers.

Budgets are another critical point. Schools operate within a very limited budget that prohibit the acquisition of the materials needed to engage in many of the STEM/STEAM programs. Even if these materials are provided free of charge, it can be restricted by the educational requirements that the teachers are forced to go through in order to implement the classes.

As a result, STEM/STEAM education gets left out and the U.S. falls further behind.

> **We need to encourage the next generation to pursue STEM/STEAM careers. In order to make this happen, they need to KNOW it exists first. Marketing is critical for generating this awareness.**

Possible negative results
When space is not at the top-of-mind, critical support is lost. Some possible negative outcomes are:
- Schools are not incorporating programs that are necessary for the future workforce to compete in the job market.
- STEM careers are not chosen.
- National space budget allocation shrinks effecting vital research.
- Preparations for asteroid collision or hostile intentions are not considered, leaving the public open to harm.
- Initiatives like a Moon landing or a space force do not have the support it needs if the public does not understand the reason for its existence.

2. Help space companies thrive.

Space is hard. Many space companies are consumed with what they are working on creating. It takes a lot of focus to make it out of Earth's gravitational pull. Marketing is not a priority in many companies. Up until recently, you had one customer to woo - the U.S. Government. This may not be the case in the near future.

Changing business model for the space industry.

Since the 2015 SPACE Act opened the doors for commercial companies, the space sector has exploded with activity. There are thousands of new players. As of 2018, over 72 countries have launched new governmental space agencies.

Competition levels are unprecedented as countries ramp up their programs and the cost for entry is reduced. Many of the space industry professionals have not had to maneuver in these waters before now.

NASA's not the only game in town anymore. European Space Agency (ESA), India, Israel, China, United Arab Emirates, and many other countries are going into space. It is going to get even more competitive as these counties pour funds into *their* space programs and into *their* country's space businesses as they reach for a piece of this powerful industry.

An example of this new competition can be seen in Moon landers. Historically, there was one solution for something like a lander. Now there are several. NASA had three companies slotted for the 2024 Moon landing. They were Blue Origin, Dynetics, and SpaceX.

Three landers are just for the U.S market. Russia, China, Japan, India, Luxembourg, and Sweden (European Union) have completed missions to the Moon.

In addition to the main countries' ambitions, there are many companies looking to go to the Moon for tourism, mining, research, communications, and more.

That is a lot of Moon landers.

The lower cost for entry into the industry has allowed many more businesses to look to the skies for emerging opportunities. As commercial space expands, so does the competition for valuable investment dollars and space contracts.

Marketing will become a necessity if you want to run in the space race.

Promote the understanding of marketing strategies and tactics through the lens of space.

What does shampoo, board games, or soup have to do with rockets or Moon landers? Marketing space is different than your regular product or service in many ways. NASA has been so successful at marketing that we are almost unaware that it is happening. In this book, I have used space-focused companies to demonstrate how marketing tactics and principles have been successfully applied within the space industry. You will find examples from some of the big names in aerospace like NASA, Boeing, and Virgin Galactic.

SETTING THE STAGE

COMPANY - *Rockets-R-Us*

Throughout the book, I use a fictitious example of a rocket launch company to describe how strategies and tactics may be applied. It will help paint a picture of the point being discussed and make it easier to understand how the strategies, tactics, and tools could be applied to your particular situation. By using a pretend company, it will give context to the application of these strategies and tactics within the space industry.

We will call them *Rockets-R-Us.* This is not a real company. If there is a company in existence with this name, it is without my knowledge.

Basic information

Rockets-R-Us is a small rocket company that transports satellite payloads into orbit. They employ 45 people, and their CEO is an engineer. This company currently focuses on non-human delivery into Earth's orbit. They are preparing for the future by developing rockets that can transport non-human cargo to the Moon within the next decade.

PART 1

CHAPTER 1

UNDERSTANDING MARKETING

How can you change the world, build a company, or establish an industry if no one knows you exist? Marketing makes you exist.

Throughout history, there have been revolutionary ideas, mind-blowing inventions, cures for disease, and products that could have made the world a better place... and they lay on a shelf somewhere gathering dust.

Why!? Those brilliant creators did not know how to convey the value of their discovery. They did not know how to speak the *right* words into the *right* ears or bring it in front of the *right* audience. In other words, they did not know how to market themselves, their ideas, or their companies.

The road is littered with creations from inventors that failed to communicate their worth through marketing.

What is marketing anyway? The American Marketing Association's official definition is "Marketing is the activity, set of institutions, & processes for creating, communicating, delivering, & exchanging offerings that have value for customers, clients, partners, & society at large."

Let's break that down.

An offering can include an idea, a product, or a service that is presented to an audience. The goal is for the audience to be swayed, educated, or convinced enough to exchange their time, effort, or money for that offering. Done correctly, it can provide a mutual benefit to everyone involved.

Good marketing builds relationships and does not feel like a sales pitch.

Space marketing is marketing that revolves around space. It is the ideas, products, and services that happen within the space industry.

These ideas include things like putting a person on the Moon, going to Mars, or mining an asteroid.

The products include things like 3D printing a human heart in lower earth orbit or, everyone's favorite, freeze-dried ice cream.

Services include things like providing rocket payload services to launch a satellite or the communication services of those satellites.

MARKETING CHALLENGES

There are some challenges that revolve around the activities of marketing. It affects most of those companies that conduct business in our world today. The following are three common challenges.

1. Marketing is misunderstood.

Marketing has gotten a bad wrap. Some of it is well deserved. When a company is only focused on fleecing its customers with an inferior product, it reflects badly on everyone.

Good marketing is NOT just a sales pitch, it is a relationship. Unfortunately, bad advertising or marketing is what annoys us the most and it is what we associate with marketing practices in general. Good marketing is often thought of using other terms such as generating awareness, outreach, or public affairs. These terms separate it away from the purveyors of the quick sale.

2. Marketing is hard.

Marketing is hard. It is a blend of art and science to hit the right message at the right moment to get the right response. If everything is done perfectly, it still may not work.
New technologies and platforms are constantly evolving how people live, work, and play.

So, how do we connect in a meaningful way AND STAY CONNECTED? This is the question that haunts most marketing professionals.

Successes and failures can be difficult to predict. Billions of dollars are spent each year in an effort to try to figure out the next viral trend. It can be frustrating because even if everything is done by the book, a campaign can still flop. On the reverse side, something offhanded or something captured on a casual afternoon can unexpectedly go viral. Even more frustrating is what works one day can cease to work on the next... literally.

The digital landscape has made it easier than ever to track the effectiveness of some marketing strategies or tactics, but not all. Some relationship-building strategies can take years to see success.

Technology innovations and events have drastically changed the marketing landscape in the past three decades. The internet connected the world and changed how people interacted, worked, and played. Smartphones amplified this new trend and social media exploded. Search engines became powerful vehicles and upset the tenuous marketing hold with algorithm changes that sided with their audiences' experience.

Then there is COVID and how it changed everything... yet again. Just when we start to figure out the marketing landscape, more changes WILL come along that will upset the status quo like 5G, Starlink, virtual and augmented reality, holograms, and a host of things that are not discovered yet.

The science that provides the ability to track and control messages has consumed many professionals. This provided a new set of activities that could be measured and orchestrated with precision. We can control the timing, frequency, and content of what our audience sees. We can measure the effectiveness of content and anticipate its reaction. All this power should provide the tools to control behaviors with science, right? Wrong.

Analytics can show a part of the story but may not represent the whole story of what your audience is thinking. The audience may not even know what they are thinking themselves! In addition, as we enter into areas that have never existed before, past facts and figures can be useless.

Some marketing tactics are based more on creativity and intuition. They can be hard to measure. How do you measure a referral from a friend-of-a-friend? How do you measure the word-of-mouth of colleagues who are chatting while waiting for a cup of coffee? How do you measure trust? How do you measure a career choice of a 12-year-old? And how much time and money do you have to dedicate to the measurement of these things? It can take years to see a relationship develop into a financial interaction, especially when you are dealing with things that can cost millions. It can be challenging to figure out what tactics worked and what didn't.

3. Marketing is changing.

Marketing can be a lot like aiming at a moving target. It is drastically affected by events and technology. Strategies that worked a year ago are obsolete today. Dedicated marketing professionals are scrambling to keep up.

The 1990s saw the explosion of the internet, 2008 was flipped on its head with the smartphone, and COVID has changed the landscape yet again. AND what about the changes that we will see with technologies that are coming such as G5 and Starlink. Hang on to your hat! You can bet another major change is coming soon.

It would be hard to predict in the early 1990s that we would have mini-computers in our pockets by 2008. All of the changes that resulted from the iPhone technology alone have changed how business is conducted for almost every industry. It is mind-boggling to think about the technologies that will be born from activities happening at this very moment.

The internet changed marketing in a momentous way as it opened up a two-way conversation with the public. For the first time, marketers had to contend with literal conversations that were

32

outside of their control as social media gave consumers a voice. It was a game changer.

Marketing will never be the same. Gone is the one-sided and demanding nature that served marketing executives for decades. People demand more in exchange for their time, money, and efforts. They demand respect and a beneficial relationship.

Changes keep happening. I would bet on new some surprises and increased competition.

How will you compete? Marketing may make the difference between success and obscurity.

Good marketing principles don't change.
A relationship with your audience is key. It doesn't matter what decade you are in, connecting with your audience is how business gets done. Companies that use people for profit usually do not make it in the long run.

The recipe is simple:
Respect your audience as people, listen to what your audience tells you, develop things that will improve their lives, and go where your audience will hear you.

It may be simple, but it is not easy.

CHAPTER 2

NEW COMMERCIAL SPACE

As the new commercial space industry explodes into a trillion-dollar enterprise, many companies will need to embrace the idea of marketing if they hope to survive. The new space game has new rules and new players.

During the Apollo era, there were only two participants in the space race, the U.S. and Russia. Now, there is a stampede of participants. The space sector is exploding with activity that is unprecedented in the past 50 years.

In 2014, Elon Musk sued the U.S. Government in protest of shutting out private companies in the rocketry bidding process. At the time, only a handful of companies were able to compete for these lucrative contracts. This event sparked a change in how space business is done.

The 2015 SPACE Act opened the doors for private and commercial enterprises to compete within the space industry. Like horses out of the gate, the space industry is attracting many new players from small companies to governmental space agencies from over 70 countries.

As a result, the increased competition is changing the space industry's business model. Marketing is crucial going forward. Companies within the space industry haven't had to rely on marketing programs like the other industries. Inventors and space entrepreneurs only had to focus on getting a contract from the only game in town, the U.S. Government.

The concept of marketing is new to some of these space companies, but it is not new to the space industry. NASA successfully engaged in marketing space the entire time. Without their efforts, the space industry would not exist.

NASA has carried the brunt of the marketing efforts since the early 1960s. It was NASA's marketing efforts that got the public to support the Apollo program. Since then, they have continued their outreach to keep space alive and excite young people to dream of endeavors and careers beyond the clouds.

We like to think of NASA's efforts as noble because people dedicate their lives to its ideals. It would diminish those choices if it was classified as sales or marketing. As a result, we use other terms take the place of the word "marketing" like outreach, public relations, and education.

Make no mistake, NASA was, and is, extremely successful at marketing. NASA has built the idea that space is something beyond just buying a trinket. They have used marketing to develop a relationship with their audience that resonates, and it feels good.

They have used the available platforms and tools in order to connect with their audience. We can learn a lot from their strategies about what worked years ago and what is still relevant today. We will look at their marketing strategies as well as the successful tactics from SpaceX, Virgin Galactic, and other companies within this book.

THE CHALLENGES OF MARKETING SPACE

Marketing has many challenges in almost every industry. There are a few that pose significant challenges to the space industry.

CHALLENGE 1: CHANGING BUSINESS MODEL

The new players in space are not dependent on grants. Billionaires, new governmental space agencies with their country's backing, new startups looking to do it better, and the creative determination of countless others will continue to expand this industry.

Even if your company relies on the grant model, it will need to have a brand worthy of consideration and will have a lot more competition vying for the contract. Your company needs to look like it deserves the award.

CHALLENGE 2: FALSE MINDSETS

When it comes to marketing, one of the biggest challenges that I see are several false mindsets that plague many company CEOs, entrepreneurs, and inventors.

False mindset #1: NASA is all we need.

False. In the past business model, the primary focus of space companies was to receive the coveted NASA grant or funding from angel investors. Little thought has been given to the activities that involve the public. It was left to NASA to build the public's view of the space industry. NASA has done a wonderful job of marketing through outreach and public affairs activities, but their role is changing as the space industry expands.

As of 2018, there were already 72 governmental space agencies in existence. These agencies are hungry to build a space economy for their respective countries who are dedicating portions of their national budgets. These countries are trying to get a slice of the pie and are encouraging local companies to reach for the stars.

As the space industry gets crowded, NASA's impact on the space industry will shrink as new space agencies grow and more countries begin their programs.

In the 2010 TITLE 51—NATIONAL AND COMMERCIAL SPACE PROGRAMS, Section 50111, it mandates, "a step-wise approach from the current regime that relies heavily on NASA sponsorship to a regime where NASA becomes one of many customers of a low-Earth orbit non-governmental human space flight enterprise."

An example of this how this process is affecting space business is regarding the running of the International Space Station (ISS). After the ISS retires, platforms in lower Earth orbit (LEO) transition from one that is government-owned and operated to one of a commercial nature.

Relying on one entity, such as NASA, to create the industry is a dangerous assumption and mindset.

False mindset #2: Space always makes the news.

False. NASA has worked hard over the past decades to get people excited about space. It is their marketing efforts that put space news in front of the public.

I want to repeat this important fact – the space industry would not be what it is if it weren't for NASA's monumental marketing efforts. They built the awareness that we all enjoy today.

That said, it is easier to garner public attention when your main event is unique and newsworthy. Each new milestone that is reached can provide newsworthy content just by existing. A new rocket launch that takes a crew up to the ISS is amazing… the first time.

Space has provided the platform to reach great heights. The excitement that is generated by achieving something great can only be sustained if you are constantly hitting new milestones and new achievements.

These great headliners will have to jockey for attention as expanding competition accomplishes great things and the news of beyond-the-orbit successes become commonplace.

Eventually the uncommon becomes common. How often do we cover space launches of the Soyuz? They have 1,680 successful launches in total, including satellites and manned spacecraft.

The Space Shuttle program became routine, and the public attention began to wane until one of them, Challenger and Columbia, would explode in tragedy. Public apathy was so great that there was little outcry when the program was canceled. U.S. space launches were crippled for a decade as a result.

Great feats of space don't always make the news.

False mindset #3: Marketing is easy.

False. Ask Coca Cola, Proctor and Gamble, McDonalds, Ford, or Sony if marketing is easy. Marketing is a shifting landscape with a moving target. Audiences move their attention to new locations like a flock of birds. The birds' movement is designed to make them less of a target. Same with an audience. People are tired of being targeted by entities they didn't invite, and they are sick of advertising interrupting their activities.

Internet, smartphones, and COVID continue to evolve the marketing environment. Technology makes it easy for an audience to avoid advertising attempts. Connecting with an audience in any meaningful way takes creativity, time, effort, and skill.

Marketing is a mix of science and art. Developing a resonance between a company and its public is not something that is acquired in one day. There are dedicated teams of skilled professionals who spend billions of dollars in pursuit of this conquering this challenge and they remain frustrated.

Space companies will need to develop marketing skills to stand out in the sea of new international companies and agencies.

False mindset #4: Marketing cheapens the science.

False. Many of the space companies are started by inventors. Some of these brilliant minds have the idea that marketing cheapens the quality of their invention and demeans it to the level of a trinket for sale. They believe that if an invention is great then everyone will want it because "it would be pure stupidity for anyone to ignore it."

If only that were true. The road is littered with revolutionary ideas, mind-blowing inventions, cures for diseases, and products that could change the world. Unfortunately, they sit somewhere on a shelf gathering dust.

I had the opportunity to begin my career as a support tenant in an environment technologies incubator. I was astounded by the inventions that I saw these brilliant people creating. These inventions could change electrical power, trash disposal, water reclamation, and more that would impact our world in major ways. Most of them never left that incubator because of the arrogance of the inventors. They believed that they did not need to market to the world because their invention should be placed on a pedestal by the world.

It doesn't matter if you have the next generation of technology that can change the world if no one knows about it. Marketing activities and efforts open the eyes and ears of the world.

Story of Nikola Tesla

Tesla was one of the brightest minds of the past two centuries. He was consumed by the secrets to electricity. All he wanted to do was study and create. Tesla had a disdain for others and thought his mind was above them. He did not care about any promotion or marketing. Unfortunately, he died penniless and unknown.

So many of his inventions and discoveries are lost. Some of his other creations were credited to someone else such as the radio. If it wasn't for the electric car named after Tesla, how many of us would know about his contributions to humanity.

As a comparison, Edison was a master at marketing. He understood his audience and presented inventions in a way that would excite them and spur adoption. He understood what the media wanted to see. His marketing acumen was instrumental in the adoption of electric light bulbs over gas lights.

Imagine where our world would be today if Nikola Tesla knew how to market *his* ideas.

A company may have the best idea, but it takes marketing for the world to see it.

False mindset #5: It has always worked this way.

Doesn't matter. New technologies and new legislation have fundamentally changed how the space industry works. The SPACE Act of 2015 opened the doors to commercial space business. New Space, or commercial space, entities demand a profit for their efforts and are working with business models that do not expect to be run by the grace of grants.

SpaceX is the most notable of this change. Within a decade, SpaceX has reduced the cost of rocket launches, changed how satellites work, and continues to push the boundaries of space business.

The expectation that the status quo will remain stable in any business is risky. The competition will force space companies to leave the established rules of engagement behind and force them to develop effective marketing strategies in order to compete. The space industry will feel this change in the force as it begins to play by the rules of other industries.

There is always a new technology or a significant event that will change how business is conducted. Those who cannot adapt will be left behind.

False mindset #6: Marketing is only sales.

False. There are several space companies that are developing innovative technologies with their only goal being "getting a NASA grant." They may see marketing as a tool that *other* companies use to sell something to the public and assume that it doesn't apply to their company.

Traditionally, space companies were focused on research, innovation, or an invention like a moon lander. NASA or individual investors were the ONLY customers. Even if this reality were true, NASA or the investors should be considered customers that still need to buy-in to the project. They need to be sold on what your company is selling. Even if the audience is only one entity, you need to market your idea to them.

Marketing makes you look more substantial and serious about your project when you present it. Marketing strategies such as a polished brand image and the right content in the right place can give a company credibility. This will make it more likely that your audience (even if it is only NASA) will take the risk and invest in your invention.

Proper marketing techniques that cater to your audience will enhance the chance that your message of value is received and will increase your chances that your message is accepted.

CHALLENGE 3: SECRETS

If no one knows you exist, how can people give you opportunities?

Guarding company secrets is one of the arguments I hear against marketing. This is a dangerous perception that can kill a company. There are very few entities that need to keep their very existence a secret. I am not speaking to them. I am speaking to the inventors that guard their project so closely that it kills the project. Marketing is essential for survival.

This DOES NOT mean that you give exclusive knowledge away to be stolen by someone with the funds to exploit it. There are other things to "talk about" in your marketing tactics that can excite your audience and build credibility without giving secrets away.

Secrets #1: NASA's secrets

During the Apollo era, the U.S. was in a fierce battle with Russia to put the first man on the Moon. Do you think there were reasons to keep everything secret? Absolutely! But NASA knew that they could not risk using secrecy as a tactic. The leadership of NASA provided the American people with information. They focused on transparency and education to provide a crucial understanding to the American public and were rewarded with the resulting support.

They used tactics that were the opposite of secrecy. These marketing tactics utilized education strategies teaching the public about how the rockets/capsules/landers worked. They provided clarity about their challenges and made it relatable by humanizing the astronauts and the scientists. They did not give away vital national secrets that would be stolen by the Russians in this important race to the Moon.

Their strategy consisted of providing a general knowledge that everyone could understand. This selected information sparked public interest and generated a sense of belonging to something monumental. NASA's marketing efforts built the dreams that would ensure the growth of the space industry for our future.

NASA's marketing tactics fed an eager public that was thirsty for knowledge and a sense of being part of something larger than themselves. This created a wide base of support and acceptance by the public that forced Congress to pass huge budgets in order to make this journey possible.

A cloak of secrecy could have provided the element of surprise to the Russians for a fleeting second, but the enlightenment of the public is what won the game. Transparency has given the space program legs to stand on and arms to reach for the future.

Secrets #2: Corporate espionage

The corporate espionage battle is fought on the frontline of almost every market. Secret sauces, shampoo recipes, fuel-efficient engines, and more innovative ideas have been safeguarded and stolen for centuries. For example, there are institutions that studied the molecular make-up of the popular cola recipe in order to replicate it and make a knock-off. It is a very serious thing and safeguards need to be put in place to protect the technology that is created within the space industry.

Don't let this be a reason not to market. Let this be a reason to market with a purpose. The BRAND means more than the product. A BRAND is built through marketing.

What if Coca-Cola was so afraid that someone would steal their secret recipe that they were unwilling to bottle it for consumption due to the requirement of listing the ingredients? Would we still have it around to enjoy?

Using the secret as a marketing tactic.

By controlling your marketing, you can create a brand that is more important that the product itself. Having this type of brand strength ensures that if someone steals the secret sauce, your brand means more than the knock-off.

Some well-known companies use their secret formula as a successful marketing tactic. The ingredients to the legendary Coca-Cola soft drink, McDonald's secret sauce, and Kentucky Fried Chicken's secret spice blend can be found on the internet. Can other companies duplicate them? Yes. But that doesn't mean that billions of people will drop their Coke to drink the imposter.

THE SIMPLE SECRET

Here is the simple secret to marketing that transcends technology and other changes to the landscape. *Establish a positive relationship with your audience that is based on respect for their needs and wants.* That's it.

This is a two-way *relationship* based on *respect*. Respect is viewing your audience as more than an animal to be milked. It is based on developing a *relationship* through honesty, integrity, and trust.

It is giving them what they need and want, not what a company wants to sell them. It is important to make this endeavor a central focus.

The marketing tools and technologies will change. Having a quality relationship with your audience is a core value that will get companies beyond those changes.

CHAPTER 3

WHO IS YOUR BRAND?

BRAND PERSONALITY

Everything is interconnected. And everything your company does is marketing.

Everything that your company does determines the brand's personality. It doesn't matter if the brand is developed with strategic thoughtful or just happens by default, it is there. When people see anything from your company or interact with its staff, they see and feel the company's personality. That personality is your brand.

The company's personality, or brand, permeates every aspect of business. It is more than pretty pictures or posts on social media.

This brand personality has a domino effect on the success of a business. The personality of your company determines its culture. This kind of culture affects your employee's satisfaction. Employee satisfaction impacts innovations, production, and is directly relational to your customer's satisfaction. All of these aspects affect the bottom line.

Company personality = brand
Company culture = brand
Company perspective = brand
Company promise = brand

Yet so many companies are dismissive of a brand's importance and its power to impact business.

YOUR BRAND IS LIKE A PERSON.

Branding is multiple marketing actions that are repeated to build awareness. Pursuing only one *type* of action isn't enough. Like a human body, it is rarely one activity that makes a body strong, but a series of different actions done repeatedly and with a purpose that builds strength. By using all of the parts, it makes the body whole. Repeated use makes it strong.

It is not just one action that makes marketing successful. Just as one hand or foot doesn't make a body whole, it is all of the parts that come together that bring a set of marketing strategies to a successful outcome.

The brand's body:

EARS

Listen to your audience. Many companies fail to listen to the very people that they are trying to convince. Traditional advertising such as ads, commercials, and billboards are failing because it is a one-way conversation. It is like someone screaming to buy their stuff. When they stop to take a breath and look around, then they are shocked to find themselves alone.

Interview your audience and ask open-ended questions. Ask them the question and then let them talk without interruption. Hear what they are telling you about their experiences with the industry, your competition, and your company.

It can be hard to hear criticism about a product or service that you have poured your heart into. If your ears and mind are open, you may discover a problem or stumbling block that you were unaware existed. This could open a new opportunity that no one has seen.

The first time I saw the power of listening was when I was working to provide STEM kits for my local schools. The kits were fun and free, but we were still getting resistance. I reached out to some teachers in order to discover what the roadblocks were. During our interviews, I found out why they were not able to use the STEM kits in the classroom.

The teachers are required to make them fit into a structure of the Uniform Academic Course Codes for our state. This required a great deal of extra effort on the part of the overworked teacher to incorporate them into their class plans.

This was a major friction point as many of the kits did not neatly fit into the codes' descriptions as they were written. I discovered that the teachers needed additional help if they were going to utilize the STEM kits in their class.

This provided an opportunity to provide additional course structure information that would provide the exact criteria that the teachers needed in order to put the STEM kits into their course plans. This service would make the kits more valuable and easier to use.

I am still shocked that the very code of education would be designed to keep STEM from being a priority. But, that is another story for another venue.

HEART

Love your audience. People can tell when you respect and love them. It shows in the developed content that is relevant, feels authentic, and speaks to them. It is apparent when the company focuses on the customer's experience compared to a customer's fleecing. Extra touches that are designed to add delight to the overall experience demonstrates purpose and thought. It is the company that cares that wins loyalty.

MOUTH

Tell lots of stories! There are few landscapes that are as awe-inspiring and spectacular as space. We have a great story to tell, so let's tell it!

Space is brimming with adventures that people want to hear about and be inspire by. It is dangerous and hard with stories that are full of bravery and monumental feats. People are aching to hear the stories of the challenges that are overcome, the dreams that push people forward, and the accomplishments of doing hard things. Space is full of all of that stuff and more.

Another key aspect of the mouth is determining who speaks for the company. Do they embody the qualities that you want your brand to represent? How do they conduct themselves? Branson, Bezos, and Musk represent their respective companies. What they do and say directly reflects the brand and their voices create their companies' brand personality.

Papa John's Pizza had a CEO that did not think before he spoke. He said a racial slur that created a severe backlash. The company removed him in order to save the brand from the controversy. The company stock prices plummeted 50% before they pulled the plug and fired him.

Choose wisely.

VOICE

A brand voice is a distinct personality that is developed within the modes of communication. It includes the language that is crafted with a unique flair that embodies the personality strategy. Keep it consistent by using selected personality traits, vocabulary, and phrases when crafting messages.

The tone can express emotion that changes the meaning of phrases. A brand's tone is how you say the words that craft the messages. Different situations may vary between audiences which require different tones.

Is the tone positive and brimming with excitement? Or is it serious, friendly, stoic? Avoid language that is demeaning, aloof, chastising, or snide. There is always a way to say something that shows respect.

Tone is defined by the consistent style of communication. It must feel true to your brand values and personality. It can be authoritative, playful, intellectual, etc. The brand voice should flavor the content that your company produces. It plays a large role in determining the brand personality and the culture of the company.

WORDS

Words are powerful. U.S. President Kennedy's words galvanize a country to embark on the enormous commitment of landing on the Moon on a hot September afternoon in 1962. The echoes of his words are still heard decades later.

Choose your brand's words and silences carefully. Plan and use them with intention and clarity. Craft your brand's word strategies with the use of stories, by avoiding deception, and be intentional with the use of silence.

Here are some DOs and DON'Ts for your brand's words:

• **Use stories.** Words can create compelling stories. Stories have captured people's imagination since the dawn of time. It is how we learn and the base of our entertainment. Storytelling passes information while generating interest and stimulating engagement.

Telling stories is one of the most powerful ways to influence, teach, and inspire. It creates connections between an audience and ideas. They relate to culture, history, and values that unify people and make them feel included.

• **Avoid lies and deception.** Never, ever, ever, ever, lie. There is not a second chance when trust is broken with your audience. There used to be some opportunities for forgiveness when there were not as many options to choose from. A company could recover from a caught lie with a news story or a flood of ads. Nowadays, there is so much noise that the apology has a small chance of being heard. In addition, the message can be blocked thus silencing any hope of communication forever.

If your company needs to lie about what it is doing, then perhaps it is time to rethink the product, service, or processes that are involved.

• **Avoid the perception of untruth.** Words can come across as false if they don't complement actions or images. This creates a sense of deception even if there isn't any. Make sure that the images and elements of your message back up your words.

• **Silence has a voice.** A respectful pause shows consideration of the idea and allows audience time to absorb the message. Silence can signal that you are listening. A hush sets the stage for an import statement or event. Awkward silences have been a powerful tool in many negotiations.

Silence can also be deadly. It can be deafening as it shouts the lack of support or a sense of not caring. Caught unprepared, it can make a company seem incompetent.

A bad type of silence can occur when you are struggling to find the right words to say. This is why a public affairs team need to exist in your company or organization and have a crisis plan in place. In times of an emergency or disaster, this department can be worth its weight in gold.

Boeing received a black eye when they failed to say anything after the 737 MAX crashes. In the span of silence, accusations grew, and blame was applied. Too much silence can make an organization look guilty or make them seem like they are trying to come up with some way to spin the event, so they don't appear to be at fault. It exposes the company culture. Trust begins to crumble. As a result of how this situation was handled, sales of the Boeing airplanes were deeply affected as orders were canceled for many of the Boeing models, not just the 737 MAX.

A moment of silence can also leave your company open to attack. This gap of silence can allow time for a competitor, enemy, or another narrative to fill the space. This can leave your company scrambling in a mode of damage control.

Be prepared to use silence and words effectively and be strategic on when to use them.

TOUCH

Touch brings an immediate awareness that triggers a heightened sense of awareness. It signals something is within an intimate proximity and the brain needs to decide whether it poses a danger to the self.

Haptic information is gathered using the power of touch. Our skin is full of sensory receptors that allow us to receive messages from experiences of texture, vibrations, temperature, pressure, pain, and other sensations. These experiences can trigger behavior and influence decisions. Touch goes right to the gut about how we feel about a person or brand.

It makes the story real. You may not be able to believe everything you hear or see, but when you touch it, it erases doubt of its existence.

The sense of touch puts someone directly into the story. It deepens communication and embeds important lessons. NASA uses this sense in its hands-on STEM programs, centers, and camps. Interactive displays and immersive experiences impact participants in ways that video and books cannot.

Kennedy Space Center has a moon rock on display that you can touch. It allows the visitors to experience its reality to the story narrative of the Moon landing. I had to touch it when I visited the center.

My brain asked whether it was worth the wait to touch what appeared to be an ordinary pebble. I stood there waiting anyway. It reminded me that there were boogers and other germs on it where millions had touched the same stone. Nevertheless, I touched it anyway.

Why it was so important to touch this rock? My heart replied that it was a connection to a dream of making the impossible possible. This act committed my belief in the reality of space and made me part of the story.

When your audience has physical interactions with your brand, what does it feel like? How is your brand utilizing the haptic sense to communicate and engage?

EYES

Space is full of beautiful images. NASA and other entities provide them to you to use. Make sure that your marketing includes stunning visuals in content and video.

Inc.com states that 65% of the population are visual learners. Images tend to stick in long-term memory better than text alone. According to the Visual Teaching Alliance, 90% of information transmitted to the brain is visual and is processed 60,000X faster in the brain than just text.

Images are more engaging and can trigger emotions. They can illustrate a process and or inspire an action. Think of the iconic image of the Earthrise from the astronauts that were on the Moon. How many lives were changed from that single image?

Posts with images and videos are 94% more likely to be read than those with text alone. Make it easy for your audience to share your images and information in your articles, videos, and posts.

This was a critical component to the success of the Apollo program. NASA understood what their audience needed. For reporters, they gave them educational manuals with images that described the facts that they would need to report accurately. NASA provided, and still provides, turnkey content for newspapers, radio, and television.

Visit https://images.nasa.gov for images, videos, and even audio to use in your content. Just remember to give them credit.

COPYRIGHT WARNING – Assume that every single image has copyright protection. It does not matter where you find it. If you are allowed to use it, it will be clearly stated. Make sure that you get permission to use images, or you could be sued.

Be seen. You cannot be everywhere to all people, but make sure you are everywhere your audience is looking. Be selective where your brand places its efforts and make sure the activities provide the most visual exposure in exchange for that effort.

SMELL

Yes- smell. One of the most powerful of the senses demands that good marketers control the experience of scent. There is a whole discipline of marketing that is focused on this powerful trigger.

Scent is a unique sense that bypasses cognitive thought and stimulates emotions in the limbic system. According to the Sense of Smell Institute, the average human being is able to recognize approximately 10,000 different odors. There are studies being conducted about how smell influences choices, thoughts, emotions, and memory.

A pleasant smell signals that the world is a positive place. It can affect mood and influence how someone feels about something.

There is an entire classification of marketing for this strategy. It is called *scent marketing*. Many savvy businesses use scent marketing like grocery stores and burger fast-food restaurants. They control the signature smell that you get when you enter. Ever wonder how a hamburger can smell completely different at McDonalds versus a hamburger at Burger King? Each restaurant develops a signature scent that is consistent in every location.

Boeing provided a perfume sample vial filled with the scent of space. I receive one when I visited their booth at the International Astronautical Congress. Astronaut Scott Kelly describes the smell of space in his book *Endurance*. I recognized the same scent on the Space Shuttle Discovery at the Smithsonian National Air and Space Museum.

This deepened the story of space for me. I keep that Boeing sample as a keepsake in my space display. This is a wonderful example of how a marketing tactic connects the audience to the company in a meaningful way that deepens the relationship.

Scent is a powerful memory trigger. We are more likely to remember a scent than something we have viewed. It provides a deeper connection to the event when a smell is attached. The positive look, feel, and aroma surrounding the brand experience can determine the level of satisfaction a customer has in the experience.

On the opposite end, don't stink. People associate the smell of a place with their experience. Moldy or old offices can take away from the professional polish of a headquarters. It can conflict with a message of "clean" when working with products. Cleanliness is critical for space operations.

CLOTHES

Clothes say a lot about a person. Hawaiian shirts and flip flops send a completely different message than a three-piece Armani suit. Your brand's clothing is depicted with its logo, website, business card, imagery, color palette, office décor, and more. It is the things people see when they look at the brand. It dresses it up and represents its personality.

Your images and messages generate a *feeling* when seen. Be purposeful when selecting the images that represent your brand and portray the feeling that you intend. Would you trust flip-flops in an investment meeting?

I hope this section gave you a clear visual of how your brand is similar to a person. Now we are going to look at how this "person" can build or destroy trust.

TRUST

Nothing matters without trust.
The best product with the best brand cannot win without trust. Trust is the key component of any relationship. Your company's service, message, and brand must radiate trust. The audience needs to trust that the job will get completed as promised and that they will be taken care of in a respectful manner.

Trust is difficult to repair once it is broken. The level of competition available makes it almost impossible to rectify. Remember, no one *has* to come back to give you a second chance.

Even small lies can have big consequences.

Sir Richard Branson took his first flight on Virgin Galactic's Unity on July 11, 2021. It was a momentous occasion full of fanfare and celebration. It represented a major milestone in commercial space as it launches opportunities for ordinary people to experience spaceflight.

The event was marred by a tiny fib. Sir Richard had entered into a partnership with Trek bicycles. As the inaugural flight video was released, there was a scene where Sir Richard road a bike to the launch area. It appeared as if that was part of the day's agenda. Unfortunately, the scene had been prerecorded and added to the reel. Virgin Galactic was called on it and had to release a letter of apology. Ouch.

It appeared to be a costly mistake. The SPCE stock price almost reached a 52-week high the next morning, but it plummeted after the story came out. Three days later, the stocked had dropped $25 per share. Was this a result of the lie? I am not sure, but it appeared that way to me.

This is a mild twist on the truth that probably seemed reasonable at the planning stage. If Sir Richard was not able to ride that day, the caravan could have been led by a group of bicyclists. It could have been an opportunity to include another promotional partnership. It did not have to be something false.

No one likes being lied to. Don't do it.

FRIENDS AND PARTNERS

Birds of a feather flock together.
You are who you associate with. This is true of brands as well. Like my Mother always said, "...the stink of bad company will rub off on you."

Does your brand have a partnership with vendors or other companies that have a bad reputation? Steer clear of associations with businesses and representatives that have disreputable business practices.

TRUST-BREAKING ACTIONS

There are other things that can break the trust of an audience. There are actions, or inactions, that can destroy valuable trust that may be inadvertently happening.

Many first impressions happen on a company's website or within the social media world. Searches are how many businesses are discovered. Before someone picks up a phone, they will research a company online to see if they are trustworthy.

Your company's online presence will be the first conversation that an audience will have with your brand.

Make no mistake, even without a phone, it is a conversation. The images, posts, and text on your website and social channels are talking loud and clear.

Does the website look like something that was slapped together in an effort to get something up? Or does it appear to be a respected line of communication that answers the audience's questions and provides education for them? Which one is your brand's image?

How much effort has been put into the facing platforms where your audience will be visiting? Is it obvious that the visitor's experience is important or is it a vanity site focused only on the company?

While I was working on this book, there was a company that I researched that had just received a huge contract for a big experiment. This contract was a substantial win for the company. But their brand did not come across as a company that wanted to increase business. Their site looked as if it was created in a day, probably for some event, and then forgotten. It was not maintained.

On their website, there were no images with the articles that they had posted as if they did not know how to insert them. There were huge lapses of time between the articles adding to the feeling that it was not updated very often.

There were a few videos on their YouTube account. These videos were not edited and contained too many moments that were not part of the story. It was filled with boring footage that could have been easily clipped by using free software or apps.

This company that I respected now appeared to be "smaller" than I believed. Trust evaporated as I wondered about its payroll struggles and its future. They appeared as a small company that got lucky.

Do you think that was the intent of their site and social platforms? I don't believe they had aimed for that kind of result. It was obvious that these online platforms were boxes that were checked off as done and then they moved on.

If you think about a brand as a person, then this brand showed up to an important meeting with a stained t-shirt and holey jeans. They ignored the people in the meeting, spoke their speech, and left. Would you give them your business? Would you trust them if they didn't even validate your presence outside the meeting?

Many companies have great products and inventions, but that is only the first step.

"But, I have great technology, idea, prototype, or [insert product, service or idea here]!" ...So what? So do a lot of other people that show respect to their audience. AND that pool of competition is growing every day.

LET ME BE CLEAR – It doesn't matter how great or revolutionary your product or idea is, you have competition. There are over 70 countries that have started space programs and China is determined to be at the top.

You must play the marketing game in order to be picked as THE answer to the clients' problems because it is no longer the ONLY answer.

TRUST KILLERS

Having undeveloped websites and social platforms can give the impression of an immature company that is trying to be bigger than they really are. In reality, the company's capabilities may be very different than perceived. Keep in mind that it is the perception that will be judged, not the reality. This will directly impact future opportunities because it undermines the trust in the ability to get the job done. I mean, after all, they can't even manage a website.

How about your brand's website and social platforms? What do they say about your trustworthiness? Are they full of tiny trust killers?

The following are some common trust killers found on websites or social platforms:

- Does the website and social platforms look maintained?
- Does it appear to be slapped together and have details that look as if a novice set it up?
- Does it speak to the audience's needs and answer their questions?
- Can a visitor find new articles with quality pictures?
- How often are articles or posts updated?
- Does the copyright date reflect the current year?
- Are there events posted that have already passed?
- Were they key players at industry events and do their articles or posts show them participating?
- Does it have a clear contact method?
- Is the phone number and physical address visible? No phone or address can make it look as if it a front for an empty business or illegitimate.
- Does it have a Q/A webpage of common questions? Are these real questions about real concerns from customers and prospects?
- Is the company caring more about hiding from their competition than catering to their potential client? Yep. This is a trust killer. People are coming to your site for research. Give them what they need to know in order to move to the next level. Designing your content to avoid

the competition is a good way of sending your prospects TO your competition.

- Can your brand be found on social media with a company profile and through mentions of followers?
- When was the last time something was posted? (post, article, image, etc.)
- Were comments or questions addressed in the posts or were they ignored because no one is monitoring the platforms?
- What is your brand's star rating on Google, Glass Door, or other online review sources?

TRUST TOOLS

There are several ways to build trust on your brand's website. Three elements that can provide trust are the use of testimonials, use of social proof, and mention of any press coverage.

People are more likely to believe a friend, peer, or colleague. People trust what their peers say over any message that a company would market about themselves. Testimonials are a trust tool. Word-of-mouth is the most effective way to bring in new clients.

Social icons on a home page give visitors a way to interact with the company. It also provides a snapshot of the interactions that a company has with customers and the public. It demonstrates what kind of service can be expected.

Mentions of any press coverage that is on the home page provides additional social proof that a company is legit.

TASKS:

- Do an audit of your company's website and social platforms. Make a list of the areas that need to be addressed.
- Design a set of questions that a visitor may have when visiting your website and social platforms. Ask someone that not familiar with the website to walk and talk their way through their journey as they search for answers to common questions. Record the process to see where the stumbling blocks are that break down trust.
- How is your brand building trust with your clients? Make a list of the things that your company does to build trust within the industry. Incorporate those things on your website and social platforms. Create articles that talk about the items and create online processes that mimic the in-person trust-building tactics that you employ.

CHAPTER 4

UNDERSTAND YOUR GOALS AND OBJECTIVES

There are many paths that a journey can take. Understanding the destination is key to avoid traveling in circles.

Having goals and objectives provide direction for the activities that your company needs to do to grow and be successful. Goals are the overarching thing that a company wants to achieve. Objectives are the steps that are taken to get there.

PURPOSE OF GOALS AND OBJECTIVES

There are some important to reasons to have goals and objectives. Here are a few considerations.

- Provide important data to indicate progress and measure effectiveness. How do you know you have arrived at your destination if you don't know where you are going? Having goals as guides help determine results and provide a valuable tool for the evaluation of a chosen strategy.
- Establish clarity for planning strategies and activities.
- Measure success and determine what strategies achieve success.
- Provide focus for all of the effort expended and keep activities on track. This increases results because no effort is wasted in recovering from a wrong direction.
- Inspire and motivate actions to push towards a common achievement. What is worse than missing that finish line by just a little bit? If you know that you are close, it motivates you to push a little bit more to reach that goal.

GOALS

A company's goals should guide actions and decisions. Goals provide a big picture of what is to be accomplished and have an impact on areas including financial results, corporate culture, and marketing strategy.

Objectives are more specific steps that need to be taken to achieve the goal. Here is an example of how they differ.

Goal: Establish authority in the commercial space industry

Objective: Vendor at five space conferences in Fiscal Year 20##.

S.M.A.R.T. CRITERIA

S.M.A.R.T. criteria give detail that aid in providing motivation and clarity for your objectives.

S.M.A.R.T. is an acronym for Specific, Measurable, Attainable, Relevant, and Timely. *Specific* refers to what is to be achieved. *Measurement* is the number of exactly what it is to be achieved. *Attainable* refers to whether it can be done in the allotted time. *Relevant* is referring to whether the objective is aligned with the main goals of the company. *Timely* is the span of time that is allotted to accomplish the objective.

S.M.A.R.T. objectives should be assigned with Key Performance Indicators (KPIs) and associated actions. A KPI can include things like analytic measurements or sales income as long as it is an important metric that accurately measures the success of the objective.

A general objective may be to *"grow our social media."* What does that really mean? It is vague and lacks impact and responsibility. It could be achieved by adding one follower or posting one piece of content. That is growth, but not what it meant by the statement.

An example of a S.M.A.R.T. objective is: *Increase Pageviews on Facebook by 10% by July 1, 2027.* This is more concrete. You know what you must do in order to achieve this objective.

By utilizing these S.M.A.R.T. objectives and establishing the KPIs that measure them, we can better understand what actions will be necessary to achieve the objective.

START WITH DATA

How do you know where you are going if you don't know where you have been?

Before you begin your journey, do an audit of where your brand is now. Grab analytics and establish the baseline. This aids in determining if the campaigns and marketing efforts are working and determine whether the goals have been met.

TASK:

Establish goals and objectives for your company. Using those goals and objectives, establish a set for the marketing strategies and set milestones to monitor their effectiveness. Understand what metrics need to be measured and compared.

A great book for understanding analytics and useful measurements is *Measure What Matters* by John Doerr.

CHAPTER 5

UNDERSTAND YOUR AUDIENCE

YOU ARE HERE FOR THEM. THEY ARE NOT HERE FOR YOU.

It is important that we begin the branding process with your audience. By having complete understanding of who your audience is, you will be able to create a brand personality that appeals to them.

When I speak of an audience, I don't mean the masses of faceless people in a dark theatre that can be easily ignored. I am referring to those *people* who are important to your brand. Those *people* are the lifeblood of your company. Those *people* who can have an impact on whether your company exists tomorrow. Those *people*.

Who is your audience?
Before we move forward into the tools of marketing, you need to be very clear about who is receiving your brand's communication. Who are you talking to?
The more you understand the "who," the better your conversation will be.

TASK:

Make a list of your audiences and rank them by level of importance. This prioritizes how you will develop content.

Examples of audiences:

- Investors
- Potential customers (This can include obvious customer types. It can also be expanded to companies that are thinking about space solutions such as cosmetics, pharmaceuticals, etc.)
- Customers
- Vendors
- Suppliers
- Employees
- Potential employees
- Legislators
- Media
- Space community
- Public (This does not mean everyone. You will have certain segments that can influence your company and the space industry.)

Note: I feel that we (the space community) have a responsibility to grow the industry as well as our individual companies.

CONVERSATION

Begin with a conversation.

A conversation is a two-way exchange of ideas and information. Most marketing that is one direction fails to connect. Talk to your audience and let them know you are listening by providing content that people want with messages, services, and products that are relevant.

Make it a priority to listen. Listen to your audience through emails, post comments, conversations in forums, as well as old fashion one-to-one conversation.

Only by listening can you create an intimate understanding of what is important to your audience. It is important to understand who they are and what they care about before you can create any content that resonates. Additionally, it is important to know where they go so you can place content where they will see it.

Afraid of what you might hear?

If it is as simple as a conversation, then why don't companies do it? Talking to people is scary. Many business owners and corporate leaders are convinced that their widget is the best idea ever made. No one wants to be told that the thing that has demanded so much sacrifice and effort may have flaws or be going in the wrong direction. It is much easier to spend money on the next marketing wonder widget guaranteed to reach that one percent rather than have a cup of coffee with an unsatisfied customer that could provide valuable insight into how to improve or expand.

The rewards of conversation

There are several rewards that can result from meaningful conversation. Knowing your audience can provide better content that resonates with targeted efficiency.

It can provide focus and makes it easier to create great content. No more wasting time guessing what to do next.

This insight provides a pathway for the deployment of that content. You now know where the audience will look for your brand's captivating content and how they will consume it. No more guessing where to spend your ad budget. In addition, you may discover that the best way to approach your audience costs a fraction of what you currently spend.

Another by-product of meaningful conversation is the evolution of your product or service. Meaningful conversation empowers you with the knowledge of how you can improve your product or service to be a better product fit. This newfound insight could also lead to an entirely new widget that serves a need that no one knew existed.

It may be one of the best investments of your time and effort.

INTERVIEW REAL PEOPLE

What are the problems and concerns of your audience? Don't guess. Don't just make something up or assume. The best way to get this information is to ask, person-to-person. Talk to your existing customers, influencers, and real people within your audience segment to get a real idea of who they are.

I guarantee that it will be surprising what you will learn.

During this process, you can learn about roadblocks and opportunities that you didn't know existed. Make sure you use unbiased and open-ended questions that will spark a free-flowing answer. Make sure that you let the participant talk and don't impede them until you are sure they have finished answering the question.

Conduct interviews with your brand's audience. Include current customers, potential customers, and customers that opted to go with a competitor. Customers that opted to go with a competitor are golden because they will highlight flaws in your company's process.

Understanding how your audience thinks will help you provide the content, service, and products that they need. It will help you provide the solutions to their problems. It will help you get to know them on a deeper level and build a stronger relationship with them.

The goal of these interviews is to gather insights that can help make their experience better. These conversations will gather knowledge about your audience that is useful and insights about their problems and pain points as it relates to your industry, buying process, or brand.

Interview tips:

- **Gather information before the interview** - Don't waste valuable time during the live interview with information that you can glean from their social accounts. In addition, this information can help focus the questions to get deeper insights during the interview process.

- **Record and take notes** – Recording the interview allows you to go back to a point and clarify it. It provides time to study their body language which you can't do while taking notes. NOTE: Make sure you have permission to record from the participant.

- **Respect their time** - Respect the time of those that you interview. Keep each interview below 30 minutes. Be punctual. Make the time and place convenient for the participant.

- **Pre-interview questionnaires** - Send pre-interview questions that can be answered beforehand. Sometimes questions need a bit of thought or checking. These questions can aid in conversations that maximizes the in-person time. Save the person-to-person interview for open-ended conversation that can lead to deeper insights.

  Pre-interview survey sample questions:
  - Who do they follow online and offline?
  - What are their preferred social media platforms or offline social activities?
  - Who are their favorites personalities and why do they enjoy their posts or content?
  - What groups do they participate in?
  - What do they like to read online and offline?
  - What are their activities at work and outside of work?

- What are their interests and hobbies?
- What are their likes and dislikes?
- What are their personal and career passions?
- What are their purchasing habits, like where and when they shop and for what items?

- **Ask open-ended questions** - Make sure to use unbiased and open-ended questions that will spark a free-flowing answer. The answers may surprise you and stimulate a new direction that was not considered before.

- **Be quiet** - Don't interrupt or offer opinions. Let them have the floor and just listen. Only speak to clarify a point or move a stalled conversation forward.

- **Post-interview** – Send a questionnaire to follow up on details that came up in conversation and need some expansion. During the interview, maybe they couldn't remember a name of a conference, or something needs clarifying.

- **Schedule future interviews with people that represent your chosen audience** – Hopefully, you have selected some participants that fit your chosen audience. Keep in touch with these people and try to interview them regularly. Sometimes things change and it would be useful to know what and why these changes happened.

This valuable information can be built over time and becomes more valuable when these conversations are done regularly. I recommend making these interviews a routine part of the marketing process.

CONDUCT USER EXPERIENCE AND USABILITY STUDIES

A usability-testing session has a participant perform tasks using a website, app, or another interface that a brand's audience may use. While the participant completes each task, their behavior is observed, and their feedback evaluated. This type of study can identify problems or roadblocks, uncover opportunities for improvement or new features, and learn about an audience's behaviors and preferences.

This is recommended to be conducted on a routine basis or when there is a big change to how the website or interface functions. Ideally, routine usability tests should be done with people that fit the chosen audience. However, it can be accomplished with a few people within the company who are unfamiliar with the website or platform.

ROCKETS-R-US APPLICATION:

Rockets-R-Us conducted a usability study for their website. They just released a new satellite bundling product and wanted to see how easy it would be for people to find it on their website. The test was recorded for future evaluations and a moderator was assigned to draw responses if a participate was stalled or needed more information.

The task was to find a new all-in-one product for companies to launch a satellite. Participants began with a search engine. They would speak aloud their thoughts and decisions as they journeyed through the process while searching for information. The moderator would ask for clarification as to why they thought of a particular search term.

Eventually, if they had not made it to the *Rockets-R-Us* website, the moderator would direct them to it to evaluate how they would find the information on the site itself.

Several new keywords and phrases were discovered that helped the team rewrite the articles to be findable, or to be found by search engines.

A user experience and usability study can help identify many roadblocks during a user's journey and can provide valuable insights to the company.

TASKS:

- Keep a running list of questions and relevant comments that your audience submits or says. This should be done with all of the customer-facing facets of your company.
- Create interview questions that pinpoint the audience's questions, pain points, concerns, and interests. Open-ended questions and conversations can lead to new ideas. After the interview, list some discoveries and possible opportunities that came out of the discussions.
- Set up interviews with representatives from your chosen audiences, potential and existing customers, vendors, etc., and ask about their experiences, roadblocks, highlights, and dissatisfactions. Take this information to design new content that addresses their problems, develop new processes that improve experiences with your brand, and create new products or improve existing products that deliver a better result.
- Conduct routine user experience studies with a representative from your chosen audiences to track how people interact with your brand.

STUDY THE USER EXPERIENCE

It is good to test your website, sales process, and any place that your brand resides to make sure possible friction is eliminated.

I would like to stress the importance of this step.

I was looking up space stuff on YouTube and got happily sucked into this series about space stations. There is a space company that had really interesting videos. They have plans for a space station that is excellent and inspirational. After consuming several hours of their videos, I visited their site and saw that they had a membership. Yay! I was intrigued and signed up. However, they had several membership levels. It began with a free level. I could not determine the differences between paid level and the free level. In addition, I could not tell if the paid version was charging the advertised amount monthly, yearly, or a lifetime. Would I be billed every month or every year? This missing information can represent a huge difference in a monetary promise. To be on the safe side, I opted for free. I would have paid for a membership just to support their vision.

Watch how users navigate your platforms. Ignoring it can be costly.

BUILD A PERSONA

From your chosen audience list, we have narrowed down the who. We have gathered real information from real people in interviews. Now we will create a persona to understand them and have them guide our marketing efforts.

A persona is a detailed description of a person who represents your brand's ideal target audience. This is a fictional person who represents the important traits and characteristics of this ideal person within a selected audience segment. The persona details include a name, demographic details, interests, and behavioral traits.

A persona builds the idea of a real person that you can get to know and have a conversation with through your content. This helps build a conversation that resonates with that audience because you **know them**.

The goal is to build a persona for each of the target audiences that you identified as important to your business. Each one will be different because each segment of your audience has unique characteristics and interests.

For example, a legislator will have a very different persona than an investor. The information and content will have different subjects and calls-to-actions.

These personas are built using demographic and psychographic information. Demographics are the facts about your audience - How old are they, where do they live, etc. Psychographics are what is important to them, what are their goals and dreams, what are their roadblocks, what do they like to do, what do they believe, where do they go for their information, etc.

Understand your audience's culture

Culture affects how a group thinks or perceives something. A group's experiences add a filter for how they solve problems, tackle challenges, and how they define happiness. Understanding how people perceive the world around them and how they think will enable your company to create a message and tone that will resonate with them.

How many personas do you need?

Great question! There is not a rule that you must have X number of personas. I would look at the audience segments and determine whether there are several different persona types that may need attention. Do you have different cultures and genders represented within the segment? A woman from India will have a different persona than a man from New York city.

How diverse your segment is will determine the number of personas that are needed.

Combine similar personas to keep it manageable. You want this to be a useful tool. Too many personas can be unwieldy and will end up on a dusty shelf.

Begin with the primary audience.

Focus on those details of an ideal person that has an influence on how your brand is perceived. Assign a name and a picture. Get to know them as people and develop your marketing efforts that speak to them.

Changing your persona

You are not married to these personas. You can always change the personas if the priorities change or there is new and better intel.

Task:

Build a persona for each important audience segment on your list. The priority audience personas should have the most detail including a name and a picture. Secondary personas don't need to be as developed as the primary one.

CHAPTER 6

SOLVE THEIR PROBLEMS

"What helps people, helps business."
Leo Burnett, an influential American advertising executive

With everything you do, approach it from your audiences' point of view. From your interviews, you should have a list of problems and pain points to unpack. What solutions can you present that solve these problems?

SpaceX is a successful company that asked questions then developed solutions to those problems. Here is a simplistic version of what that may have looked like.
"What is the problem?" Space is expensive.
"So how do we solve it?" Make rocket launches cheaper.
"How can we make them cheaper?" Reuse them.
And so, they made rockets reusable.

They didn't stop with rockets. Everything that they do solves a problem from legislation hurtles to more powerful engine components.

Be the answer to your audiences' questions

When constructing your list of questions, it does not have to be just about your company's services but can include questions that occur earlier in the customer journey. What happens before they get to the subjects of your category?

Rockets-R-Us application:

For example, *Rockets-R-Us* could delve into areas where people are looking for solutions for problems where satellites are just one of several options. Content could be developed that shows the benefits of using a satellite, where and how to get a satellite made, components of a satellite, orbital considerations, etc.

When they have developed their satellite with your help, they will have developed a relationship with your brand and trust it – *even if they have never had a real conversation with your company.* They will value trust as an important deciding factor even if your company's services cost more than your competitor. That trust will be worth the extra cost.

This is where having a persona to "talk to" becomes a valuable tool. Each type of audience will have different concerns and questions.

Use marketing to shine a light on the answers. Those answers will then shine a light on your brand. It is a circle that generates momentum.

In the example for *Rockets-R-Us,* they have several audiences that they will need to generate a "conversation." Each one will require a different content discussion.

One audience is with their investors. *Rockets-R-Us* will need to focus on facts and figures with their vision of how the company will win in the future. The investors will need proof that *Rockets-R-Us* is a safe bet and that their investment will earn money. Content and presentations will need to speak to the investor's needs. Content for this audience could include online and offline professional presentations, video tours, prospectus booklets, annual reports, and website articles.

In contrast, a customer audience looking into launch services will need a whole new set of content that speaks to them such as services and bundles that can help them achieve their goal of getting their satellite into orbit. A lot of their research into the company happens online. Content for this audience could include website articles, training videos, testimonials, white papers, case studies, and a presence at industry conferences.

The conversation will be different when presenting your company culture to a prospective employee. An engineer considering *Rockets-R-Us* will want to be reassured that if they come on board, the company will be around, and it will be worth the risk to move if they need to relocate.

In addition, they will want to know that their talents and ideas will be valued. They will want to feel like they are a part of something great. Content for this audience could include positive articles from about the company culture, testimonials from current and past employees, good reviews on platforms such as Glassdoor, and provide the company's plan for success.

TASK:

Make a list of your audiences' problems.
Additional places to look include the comments section on article posts or social posts from your content as well as other companies. Industry forums could be a great place to answer questions from your target audience and create awareness of your brand while providing new inspiration for your content.

Take note of the platforms and places that the audience will look for the answers they seek.

CHAPTER 7

BRAND STORY

Your brand has a story. It can be a story that you control or one that is assigned by default. Either way, you have one. Is it interesting? Does it resonate with your audience?

Your brand's story defines the brand's personality. Is it a charismatic character that everyone wants to be around or a boring individual sitting in a corner with their arms crossed muttering about how no one ever talks to them?

Your company has a brand story whether or not you are conscious of it. You can control it and make it work for you. OR you can let the brand story unfold on its own and clean up after it.

Building blocks of a story

Stories make everything more engaging from marketing content to board room presentations.

A great book for understanding how great stories can be developed is Donald Miller's *Building a Story Brand*. I refer to his recipe for a story because it is the best way I have found to describe the structure of a story. Donald's story structure is as follows:

"A CHARACTER who wants something encounters a PROBLEM before they can get it. At the peak of their despair, a GUIDE steps into their lives, gives them a PLAN, and CALLS THEM TO ACTION. That action helps them avoid FAILURE and ends in SUCCESS."

The CHARACTER is the hero of the story. This is not your brand, but your audience. They are looking for a solution that helps them

85

survive and thrive. Your brand is the GUIDE of the story. The PROBLEM is the villain of the story.

Many companies mistakenly take the point of view of the hero. They make the story about them. This leaves the customer out of the story. If you think about the role of the hero, you may not be so quick to take it on. The hero is plagued with doubt and attacked by problems. They are ignorant of what they should do and are usually reluctant to take on the quest. Does this sound like the character that your brand should be? This is your audience's role in the story.

Your brand is the role of the MENTOR and GUIDE. Your brand is the expert that knows the way to the holy grail of solutions. Your brand supplies the answers and tools to your hero, the audience, that they need in order to accomplish their quest. Your brand shines a light on the path that the hero should take to provide safe passage to their quest's end.

The villain of the story is your audience's problem that blocks the hero's way. What are the issues that they need help with? Where do they need guidance? The earlier in the journey that you can help solve these issues, the deeper your relationship will be with your brand's audience.

Rockets-R-Us application:

Let's take the *Rockets-R-Us* launch company example and break it down. The HERO and the CHARACTER of this story is a new satellite company, *Sats-R-Us*. I know- great name, right?! It is purely fictitious) They need their satellite in orbit (the QUEST).

The PROBLEM, or villain, represents the audience's ignorance of the process, regulations, gravity restrictions, orbital needs, and cost. What information and tools can you give them to make their journey more successful and ends with the quest fulfilled?

Sats-R-Us is in the beginning stages of building a satellite. They are frustrated with the information that they have been able to find about how to get their precious satellite into space. The villain, Ignorance, blocks the passage of their satellite's launch.

There are so many variables that *Sats-R-Us* doesn't know. Many options have features that don't make any sense to the novice satellite company. What size rocket do they need? What is the general cost difference in fuel types? *Sats-R-Us* need this information before they begin to build their satellite to ensure it is within the requirements. The project is halted until they can find this elusive information in the CLIMAX of the story. All is hopeless. Who, *oh who*, will guide them in this complicated journey!?

Rockets-R-Us is the GUIDE, or mentor of the story. They have all kinds of articles and videos to help would-be satellite orbiters to understand the process. They have an online chat where people can ask questions, downloadable plans and checklists, events with speakers with other companies that are going through the same struggles, and they make all kinds of educational videos available with no strings attached. Their content attacks Ignorance by providing directions and answers to the questions of the hero, their audience.

When the hero is ready, *Rockets-R-Us* asks for the opportunity to bid in a CALL-TO-ACTION. They tell *Sat-R-Us* about the bundle of services that can take them through the entire launch process including help with building their satellite and software to help track it once it is in orbit. Information about this bundle was peppered throughout their content with a convenient button for when *Sat-R-Us* was ready to begin a relationship. It takes them to a page with the next steps and contact information to begin their journey to space.

Even though *Rockets-R-Us* is not the lowest bid, the satellite company chooses them because they know that *Rockets-R-Us* understands their needs and they trust them.

The satellite is launched, and *Sat-R-Us* lived happily ever after.

Having a brand story established makes developing content easier and more productive. Once you know your brand's story and its place in it, it becomes easier to creating marketing content that speaks to your customer's needs and provides clarity about how to position your brand as the expert. It can provide a base from where ideas flow.

APPLY IT

What are the villains, or problems, in your audience's quest?
How can your brand guide them to success?
What does your company currently offer that provides solutions to those problems?
What services can your company add to address those problems?

Build on an established story

Television, movies, sci-fi novels, and games have primed the public for exploits into space. Many of these fans turn their dreams of space into real companies that reach for the stars.

Build on a story that people already know and has already been successful.

Note: Be careful of copyright infringement and plagiarism.

Elon Musk uses this storytelling tactic for several of his companies. The Falcon rocket pays homage to the Millennium Falcon in Star Wars. The story is constantly reinforced when possible. At a presentation on Sept 28, 2019, he used a slide for comparing sizes between rockets. The Millennium Falcon was shown as a visual homage to this iconic spaceship. It reinforced the SpaceX story and linked the Star Wars fans to their dream of space exploration.

Star Wars fans love the story of the sagas. They have an emotional connection to the story and long for a time where they can be part of the space adventures. SpaceX inserts itself into the story and becomes the hope for that dream's fruition.

Elon Musk was careful not to name his rocket Millennium Falcon because that could run aground for copyright issues. The term "falcon" is a common bird and did not step on any toes while playing to the Star Wars connection with his audience.

Tesla is another example of an existing story that captures the emotions of its fans. Tesla was an inventor who sought the secrets of electricity. He struggled against the giants of his day to make better electric things. The electric car that bears his name battles against the large automakers to make better cars. The story resonates with the brand.

Elon Musk was able to build a third story when he brought these two brands together. A mannikin named Starman wearing a spacesuit and driving a cherry red Tesla Roadster was shot out of the cargo bay of the historic February 2018 Falcon Heavy test flight. The test launch payload requirement could have been satisfied with a concrete block. By adding the sportscar and its driver, it generated content and conversation for both brands that have lasted beyond the initial launch. Starman still cruises around space on an orbit around the sun that flies by Mars.

A fourth story was highjacked with hidden surprises within the car itself. For those fans who pay attention to details, the "Don't Panic" sign sits on the dashboard of the Starman's car in a nod to the popular book, *Hitchhiker's Guide to the Galaxy*. Residing in the glove compartment is a copy of the book itself.

Adding these types of Easter eggs into a brand can add delight and drive people to look hard at your content in hopes of discovering the secret messages. Those fans that get the pop culture reference will feel special because it feels personal. It initiates them into a tribe that "gets it."

The clever use of Easter eggs doesn't stop there. Many small details are built into the SpaceX/Telsa story from the design of the new spacesuit to the stamp Made on Earth by Humans. These details symbolize the SpaceX's story of interplanetary travel.

The details resonate with the everyday person that space is for them, not just scientists and government. Everyone can relate to the casual pose of Starman enjoying the ride while the radio plays his favorite song. The entire tableau embodies the excitement, the coolness, and the dream of going into space. The scene makes it real and sparks hope.

The car was a perfect fit for the story of both brand's goals as they change the status quo and break free of the traditional business models in space, automobiles, and marketing. It extends the conversation for both brands and the industries that they represent.

APPLY IT

What stunt can your company add to an event that will be fun and add meaning?
What hidden surprises can you add for your fans to discover?
What pop-culture reference can you add to your brand's story?

CHAPTER 8

VISUAL ELEMENTS OF YOUR BRAND

KEEP IT CONSISTENT

Consistency is a vital component of trust. A brand needs to be consistent in how it sounds, feels, and looks. If a brand looks different each time someone visits, it degrades trust...*that's if they remember you at all.* **It takes 5 to 7 impressions for people to remember a brand.** That is the official number at the moment. I believe it is higher. Each time you dramatically change your brand, it resets the impressions to begin all over again.

When your brand's colors, images, and messages are consistent, it deepens the impression with your audience because it *feels* the same.

The lifespan is different for each of your brand's visual components. The logo has a long lifespan. Colors can be updated more frequently. The main message stays consistent through time. Content styles and campaigns have shorter spans.

Each element that is consistent deepens the touch or impression. Only change these components **when they cease to be effective.** This is an expensive endeavor and should be a strategic move when it happens. I have seen many businesses that wanted to change this vital connection because they were bored of it. That is not a good reason.

LOGO

Only change the components of an identity when they cease to be effective.

Coca-Cola has had the same logo for 130 years. It has seen minor tweaks over the years, but their logo still works for them and is relevant. In comparison, UPS had four major updates to their logo during the similar span of time. They updated it when it began to hurt the company's image by making them look outdated. It was not a complete departure as they still kept the elements of it intact. This ensured that they still continued to look like the UPS brand.

Time to update

If it is time for your logo to be updated, you don't want to erase all of the past exposure by looking like a new entity. Keep important elements. UPS kept their shield and their brown color.

Some space brands have been around for decades. A few of these need to be updated. Space is represented by advances and discoveries. If your logo looks like it was created in the 1970s, it is time to update.

Companies will struggle to attract a younger demographic if the brand looks old and outdated. Unfortunately, sometimes there is a great emotion tied to the old logo and it can be difficult for the founders to let go of their "baby" and change. Don't be so attached that you cannot update when it is necessary.

Having an outdated logo can hurt your organization. It would be like having an old black and white television and wondering why no one wants it. Even though your product may be high-tech, **you're not high-tech if your logo or identity says you're not.**

Sometimes a simple color change can freshen up a logo. Maybe it is bolding the lines or tiny elemental changes that can give it new life. Let strategy and need dictate these changes.

Components of a logo

There can be two parts to a logo. An icon that accompanies the brand's name is referred to as a logo bug. Logo bugs can be recognizable on their own such as the Nike swoosh or the Starbuck's mermaid. The type or font solution gives the name of the company or organization a distinctive look and style. Some logos do not have a logo bug and stick to just a type solution for their company name.

Your brand's logo should have a story behind it. One of my favorite brand images is Firefly Aerospace. They have a high-tech version of a lightning bug for their logo bug. The CEO named the company Firefly because "he imagines a time when there are so many rockets launching that they will look like fireflies in the night sky."

Trademarks

Logo bugs have diminished in importance. You can affix one to your name from stock images along with hundreds of other companies using the same image.

Sharing an image with other companies makes it impossible to trademark. Trademarks protect your company from others that may want to snatch your business or highjack your marketing efforts.

Having your brand trademarked is a good way to protect your image. If your brand does not have this protection, another company can gain the trademark and then sue you for trademark infringement... ***even if your brand was here first.***

There are many levels of trademark protection from the state level to the international level. Contact a trademark attorney to get more information.

COLOR PALETTE

Colors tell a story. Color improves brand recognition by up to 80%. Colors stimulate emotion, project messages, and provides symbolism. One to two colors are generally depicted in a logo and the overall identity.

Your branding should have a designated color palate with 5-7 colors. The other colors should complement the two main colors. These colors are used in the elements that represent your company, website, campaigns, social media posts, etc.

Color can trigger an emotion and leave a lingering feeling. What does your brand *feel* like? Is it daring, sophisticated, or classic?

One of my favorite color combinations in the aerospace world is Firefly Aerospace mentioned in the earlier section. They use a bright green against a very dark blue background. The green glows like ... well, like a firefly against the night sky.

The *Pantone Guide to Communicating with Color* by Leatrice Eiseman is one of the best books that I have found for the symbolism of color. She states in her book, "Color is the most instantaneous method of conveying messages and meanings."

Colors can alter their meaning with intensity or saturation. The different shades of a color can depict the strength of its color, such as deeper blues increase authority. As the shade migrates with other colors, it can change the meanings, such as a healthy true green moving to a sickly yellowy green.

Darkening any color increases its power. The different color combinations can create different moods. Most logos are a combination of two colors, not counting the background. Regardless of your color choices, you will need versions that work on a white and dark background.

Traditional western color symbolism:

Black: space, dramatic, sophistication, luxury, death, ominous, empty, powerful, mysterious, night, elegant
Dark blue: night sky, authority, dependable, calm
Mid to light blue: life, planet, water, peace
Red: action, stimulates appetites, intensity, power, rocket fire, love, danger
Orange: Mars, rocket fire, vibrance
Yellow: Sun, appetite stimulant, light, warmth, rocket fire
White: Moon, stars, clean, pure, simple, light
Green: health, life, nature, emerald, money
Brown: safety, earth, dwelling, chocolate, durable
Purple: creative, spiritual, sensual, royal

Color in culture

Color has deep meaning and symbolism. Color can mean something completely opposite from one culture to another. For example, in the American culture, black symbolizes death but in Japanese culture, white symbolizes death. Color can trigger an emotion. When crafting a campaign that embodies an emotion, it will need to have the correct colors to create the impact.

In western countries, red is not something you want to see when dealing with money. In contrast, the Chinese use red to symbolize wealth and money.

If you will be dealing with other countries, (and everyone in space should be) keep in mind what your color may mean to that audience. Fortunately, some colors are universal for the space industry. The black of space and blues of our planet are universal in their meaning.

Avoid trendy colors

If you decide to update, don't go with a look that is too trendy and will grow outdated quickly. Try to choose colors that will some staying power as your brand's core identity. You may be stuck with them for a while. Coca-cola has used red for over 130 years.

Back in the early 2000s, a major car company rebranded. They chose a trendy bright green, a bright blue, a mid-gray tone, and orange as their color palette. It was a popular color combination that year...and only that year. It was a difficult color combination to work with because there was not enough contrast between the colors. They were too similar in frequency. When a frequency is the same, the colors would look identical to a person who was color-blind.

In addition, the colors were bright and faded easily in the sun. By the end of the summer, signs were unreadable. This was a bigger problem than just getting new business cards. They remodeled hundreds of dealerships across the U.S. to match the fad color scheme. Within about two years, the colors fell out of favor and the newly refurbished dealerships were instantly outdated.

On the flip side, you need to update the colors if they fall out of popularity and **cease to be effective**. Many times, a color can be updated without a lot of pomp and circumstance. For example, Walmart updated its blue and yellow to freshen up their brand.

There are plenty of trending colors that can stand the test of time. Choose wisely and test them out with your audience before you commit massive spending in a rebrand.

CHAPTER 9

CONTENT

CONTENT MINDSET

Content needs to be developed with your brand's audience in mind. When content is crafted with their needs and experience at the core, it will be relevant and resonate with them. It has to be real and meaningful, not a sales message. They have to see and feel the authenticity in their lives.

YOU ARE HERE FOR THEM. They are not here for you.
When you develop content, think about the needs and wants of your audience first. Dedicate your company and your content to providing solutions for your audience. If you do this, you may have a chance of having your content consumed, shared, and enjoyed. You are here to fill those needs, regardless of whether your audience is NASA or the public.

Many of the strategies include several tactics that create a recipe for success. It takes a series of marketing tactics that build momentum to lift a company.

Jim Collins equated this to a flywheel in his book, *Good to Great.* He describes the Flywheel Effect as, *"In building a great company or social sector enterprise, there is no single defining action, no grand program, no one killer innovation, no solitary lucky break, no miracle moment. Rather, the process resembles relentlessly pushing a giant, heavy flywheel, turn upon turn, building momentum until a point of breakthrough, and beyond."*

Be relevant and resonate

Create content that resonates and is meaningful. It takes dedicated and thoughtful hours creating messages that resonate and stirs emotion within your audience. Once you tune into their frequency, they will respond. Understanding their wants and needs can transform your brand's relationship with them.

Inform. Inspire. Entertain.

There is one secret for creating engaging content. It needs to tell a story that informs, inspires, and/or entertains. Content that is not inspirational, helpful, or entertaining gets skipped over or disregarded.

This means that a picture of the product with BUY ME splashed across the top does not meet this criterion and is a waste of effort. Where is the story, emotion, information, or entertainment value in a post like this?

GE understands this concept and delivers. One of my favorite GE series, *In the Wild*, employs one of my favorite marketing strategies. GE used video to make their information entertaining as well as informative and educational. It demonstrates its product in a way that is not a commercial. This strategy brings partners along for additional audience exposure.

GE In the Wild is an informative and entertaining YouTube series created by GE Theater and IMG to go behind the scenes of GE with new locations and innovative products from airplane engines to medical MRI machines to wind farms. They used two television personalities already established in the science and entertainment field. It is hosted by Adam Savage from Mythbusters and Alie Ward, CBS's science correspondent from Innovation Nation. They go behind the scenes of GE's leading facilities to explore GE's industrial innovation in a 12-part series.

The goal of this series is to demonstrate the science behind GE's industrial products in an entertaining way. By using established influencers, they were able to have acquire social proof as well as talent. GE has over 217k subscribers on their YouTube Channel with over 7.3 million views for this series (11 of 12 videos posted) ranging from 397k to 1.6m views per video as of April 2021.

It was successful in demonstrating the diverse product lines within GE's portfolio and promoting their innovative products while entertaining an audience. In addition, it positions GE in a positive light for investors, potential employees, and future engineers and scientists.

The choice of hosts was a perfect balance of young and old(er), male and female, and encompasses a broad range of demographics with people of influence. Adam Savage is an older man that can relate to several age groups. Mythbusters demographics were 66 percent male ages 25-54. (Good, 2010). Alie Ward is a millennial representative on CBS's Innovation Nation that appeals to young viewers and their families. (Litton, 2019).

GE in the Wild is just one of several YouTube campaigns that GE has created to introduce, promote, and explain its innovative products. Other GE video playlists include *GE Unimpossible Missions, GE Innovation & Invention, GE DRONEWEEK, Trade Wars, GE Additive Paradox*, and *GE Employee Takeover.*

Many of these series include highlighting business partners while integrating the GE product line. This is a great strategy because it amplifies the potential audience of the video by including the partners' audiences. It enhances the potential to be found on search engines as it expands the keywords that are included with the partners' business. It provides additional promotion by the partner as they house the video on their web pages, sending out news releases, and posting on social platforms. The partner can cover some of the expenses of creating the video as well.

It is a perfect example of what marketing can be.

Let it shine.

Don't hide your information. Get it out there. Your audience will reward you when you provide the information that they need in order to make the decisions that help them survive and thrive.

All of your brand's content should position your company as the expert in your niche. As the expert, there will be more opportunities for free promotion. Other companies and organizations will refer to your information when discussing the subject. You may be called for news segments and articles for your expert opinion. And as the expert, you may be asked to be a guest speaker at conferences and podcasts. You may even be referenced in books and articles such as this one.

A book that I recommend is *They Ask You Answer* by Marcus Sheridan. In his book, on his website, and in his talks, he discusses the importance of providing information to your audience. He discusses his experiences of sharing his information and how it saved his business. If that wasn't enough, this tactic made his company one of the highest earners in the U.S. in the swimming pool industry. It is a great story and a great marketing strategy.

In this day-in-time, people will research extensively before they ever reach out to engage. I believe this is because they don't want to be hounded by calls or emails from the companies they are researching. What's worse is when those companies sell our information, and we get spammed to death. We will learn all we can before we open those flood gates.

WARNING: *NEVER buy a list.* One bad email on the list and email servers will ban your emails. ALL OF THEM! This includes the existing client emails that you are currently using. Some "snare" emails are placed as traps to catch harvest bots (which are bad ones) and are planted on random websites. Harvest bots are programs that troll the internet looking for emails that they can "harvest" for lists that they sell to companies. You do not want to use that list because it could blacklist your company.

Culture in content

Culture is the way we live our lives. It is defined by our customs, traditions, languages, values, beliefs, history, and ideology. Cultural customization in marketing is tailoring a message to appeal to a certain segment of people that utilizes elements they find relevant.

Culture can be derived from many sources. It can stem from religion, location, ethnicity, employment, pursuits, and ideas. For example, space is a cultural mindset. These facets can be broad like the United States or can be finetuned to minute subsets like a specific school in the Bronx area of New York City.

Marketing strategies should use elements that include language, color symbolism, symbols, or things pulled from their experiences. These things say, "I understand you" and we are part of the same tribe. These elements should be used to appeal and connect to an audience online and offline.

Culture affects how a group thinks or perceives something. The common reality that a group experiences together filters how they solve problems, tackle challenges, or how they define happiness. Understanding how people perceive the world around them and how they think enables the creation of a message that will resonate with them.

Understanding the culture of your audience plays a main role in determining the message, appropriate colors and symbols, as well as the most effective medium or platform to launch the message. This understanding flavors the content. Only by deeply understanding a people can you strum the emotional cords and become relevant to them.

Be authentic

It is dangerous to use tactics without heart. Make no mistake, people know when they are being played and fleeced. The same words from a source that doesn't care, will fall flat. Love your audience and care about their struggles.

Create excitement

When you understand your audience, it is easier to tell a story and touch on an emotional nerve that resonates and generates excitement. A good story uses both words and visuals to create a message.

Deliver value

Content needs to deliver value to your audience. It needs to inform, educate, stimulate, inspire, and entertain.

Benefits versus features

It is important to focus on the benefits of your product, service, or idea when having a conversation, or marketing moment, with your audience.

What is the difference between a benefit and a feature?
Features are the details of what something is. Take a muscle car as an example. A V-8 engine is a feature. The power and speed that it produces that allows the driver to feel exhilarated is the benefit. Benefits are what people care about when they choose a car.

Another example of a feature would be a 12-gallon gas tank in a sedan. The benefit would be the distance a driver could drive between fill-ups and the freedom that benefit provides.

Benefits are the outcomes or results that an audience will experience by using your product or service. It focuses on answering the question, "what will it do for me or my company?" This is what will convert a prospective customer into an actual customer.

There is a looooong list of facts and figures that *Rockets-R-Us* could spout about their engines, fuel, and capacity. All those features are meaningless unless the audience understands how those things will benefit them. Does a customer really care about how much capacity the rocket will carry or the type of fuel it uses? Not really. They want to know that it will get their satellite to orbit safely and affordably. Period.

Capacity can be related to price. Unless there is context to how it affects the cost or timeline of their payload, it will not mean anything. Make your content relate to your audience's benefits and concerns.

Customers will choose a payload supplier based on how the company benefits them and their company. How can you help them navigate the process? Where does it launch from and how does their satellite get there? How long is the wait time? What happens if the rocket blows up? ...with their satellite?!

Focus on the benefits that your company can provide your customer. That's really what they want to know.

TASK:

Make a list of the features for your company's product or service. Answer "So what? What does that mean for the customer?" Verify these answers with your audience.

CONTENT STRATEGIES

Content is an asset. It can build your brand, stimulate conversation, provide fodder for search engines, and promote your company.

Content considerations:

Below are some things to think about when it comes to your content.

- Select the top platforms that will give your brand the most visibility by your audience.
- Create content that will resonate on the chosen platforms.
- It should include images and prose that tells your brand's stories.
- 99.9% of content should have quality verbiage AND a quality picture that is consistent with the brand.
- Content should focus on the benefits for your customers and add another layer of why they should choose your company over your competitor.
- Reduce any friction to your company's content. Make it easy for your audience to find what they are looking for.
- Share the love. Include other entities like vendors, business partners, and industry influencers. When your content includes others, it is more likely to be shared by them.
- Some content can benefit from monetization such as videos.
- Use keywords to boost findability.
- Track the content's analytics to monitor what works and what needs work.

When you have a good idea for a piece of content, see if it works in other forms. An article's idea can grow into other forms such as an infographic or video.

Rockets-R-Us content example

Rockets-R-Us is unveiling a new rocket that can go into Lower Earth Orbit (LEO) for 25% less than standard rockets. They write and publish a news release announcing the new rocket and its capabilities.

Most companies would stop with a single news release. Don't be like most companies.

But, *Rockets-R-Us* doesn't stop there! They create a big event and invite the media, government officials, and business leaders. They arrange for five of their major customers to talk onstage about what their satellites are doing and future projects.

By having more businesses involved, it generates a buzz about the event and expands into a series of articles, posts, and video interviews about their guest speakers' stories. The guest-speaking customers benefit from some extra marketing exposure which makes conducting business with *Rockets-R-Us* more appealing for those watching.

The company fills the audience with their friends, families, and colleagues which elevates the importance of being seen at this exclusive event. Each guest is encouraged to share the event content. The content highlights the *Rockets-R-Us* partners, and it encourages even more shares.

The event is streamed live on the social platforms. Between the guests' speeches, a commentator highlights the rocket, snippets of the history of the company, and interviews the guests like a red-carpet affair.

Rockets-R-Us has the new rocket in the middle of the room with a cover over it. For the finale of the event, there is a countdown that builds the level of excitement as the cover is whisked off to reveal the new design of the rocket that is dramatically lit by lights. A beautiful graphic gracefully curves around the barrel of the rocket.

More articles and social posts after the event show the fun that guests had during the gala. It highlights the companies that spoke and those A-list people that were in attendance. All of this content includes a link to their company, of course.

Then we have the maiden voyage. Articles, video interviews, and posts leading up to the launch of the new rocket includes the companies of the payload and their stories (with their approval). This content highlights the clients' stories and what the satellites mean for them.

Several media outlets were present at the event and the launch and featured *Rockets-R-Us* in their programming. Several other papers ran the articles that *Rocket-R-Us* sent to them.

Marketing income: *Rockets-R-Us* monetized their videos and generated $10,000 from over a million views.

Possible results: Sales increase and the waiting list expanded for payload services. Several potential customers that were at the rocket reveal commit soon after the event. Other future customers receive posts, watch the videos, and read the articles. The educational videos on the website see a dramatic increase which increased their sales leads.

Which is a better marketing strategy?
You can see from this example that a single event can have very different outcomes if a company can step out of the daily grind and view the moment from a marketing lens. Adding the focus of your customer can generate even more content sharing because it has gone beyond a simple sell tactic of "here is our stuff, buy it" model.

You can choose to have one press release and hope that it gets a reporter to pick it up OR you can make it more with creative marketing strategies that generates a world of content and goodwill. This single event can have a multitude of content outlets and energy built around it.

This is how good marketing can impact your brand's awareness, your reputation, and your bottom dollar.

Each piece of content has the potential to grow onto other platforms. There is an opportunity for one article, video, or post to generate ten or more pieces of content through other channels.

NUTS AND BOLTS OF CONTENT

Here is a list of common content examples:

- Articles, blogs, press releases
- eBooks, white papers, case studies
- Social posts such as video, infographics, images, story highlights, etc.
- Videos for social snippets, event highlights, education, and training
- Programming such as television and podcasts
- VR/AR experiences

Focus on images and prose that tell a story. Make sure that all prose and pictures have the tone and voice of the brand.

The more consistent the brand elements, the deeper the connection.

COMMON ELEMENTS

Branding

Keep logos, color palettes, audio signatures, and content styling consistent. The more consistent the elements, the more of a chance your brand has at being remembered. Each time a brand is changed, it resets the number of exposures and starts over. Depending on the severity of the change, it can completely erase any previous views.

The Rule of Seven is a common adage. It states that a brand's ad needs to be seen seven times before someone will buy. I believe this is an outdated rule and it requires more than just exposures to initiate a response in our modern world. It takes repeated connections to an audience to elicit a response. I recommend reading: *Marketing Rebellion* by Mark Schaefer for more insight into this subject.

This rule does not mean that you should churn out stale and old content just to be seen. Some aspects need to be fresh and new.

My rule of thumb: Only change branding elements when they cease to be effective. Do not change just because you are bored of it.

Consistency in elements encourages the development of trust. An inconsistent brand can signal a lack of professionality and can impact a brand's trustworthiness. Trust is a crucial factor. Without it, a brand cannot succeed.

GRAPHIC ELEMENTS

A strong brand or campaign will have similar graphic elements and styles. It provides a feeling of the brand.

Brand Images

Images are an integral part of the story. They bring the audience into the scene and connect them to the story.

Images transport the viewer into the scene. Words provide context and weave a story. *For example:* Imagine a picture of a space capsule surrounded by the inky blackness of space. As a viewer of the picture, you place yourself with the capsule and you are ready for the story to unfold.

Scenario one – "As we broke free of gravity, the wild ride suddenly stopped, and the crew experienced a new peace in the arms of space."

Scenario two – "As we approached the capsule, we had no idea what we would find. Communications ceased a week ago."

Same picture, different context, and drastically different emotions.

"A picture is worth a thousand words."

This adage relates to how an image, video, and a graphic can convey a message better and quicker than words alone. Most of the public are visual learners. Images on Facebook get 352% more engagement than posts with links only. People generally ignore posts that are text only. Articles with images get 94% more views.

Photos and graphics need to:
- Tell a story.
- Capture people's attention then keeps it.
- Deliver a convincing message that is authentic and feels genuine.
- Keep a style and tone that is consistent across the brand's identity.
- Represent the brand's personality and voice.
- Resonate with the audience and connect with them.
- Identify emotions or sentiments such as longing, curiosity, inspiration, etc.
- Avoid looking dated.
- Avoid low-quality images.

Develop a library of images for your company that are good quality and tells your brand's story. Real images about real events, real people, and real stories work best for communications. Sometimes this is not feasible, or you need something to augment the library. Pictures, videos, and images can be found through online stock photo/image sites and are available at reasonable prices.

CALL-TO-ACTIONS

"Pat your head. Come on everyone, pat your head." This is how I would begin my call-to-action marketing sessions. I would pat my head and tell everyone to pat theirs. Then I would ask them, "Why are you patting your head?" followed by "Because I asked you to do it."

This displayed the power of a call-to-action even when an audience did not know why. It is also important to note that it generally took asking more than once and then followed by a silence to let them know that the request was genuine. After the first few people began, it took a few moments after the ask for it to swell as the crowd began patting their heads. Many people did it only because everyone else was doing it. This demonstrated the power of the ask.

What do you want your audience to do? They have looked at your post, watched your video, listened to your podcast, now what? It may seem obvious what you want them to do, but you have to say it. Saying the words causes action. Implying the words causes inaction.

Many effective call-to-actions can be as simple as "watch the next video," "read more," or the legendary "buy now."

Be very clear about what the call-to action is on every piece of content. This is as important for the content developer as it is for the audience. It defines the content's purpose and intent.

It doesn't have to be a sales-focused call-to-action. One of the best call-to-actions was the "Think different" campaign for Apple. In two words, they resonated with their audience and demonstrated that they understood who they were.

Were they selling difference? Yes, they were. Their audience thought that they were different and by owning an Apple product, it made them part of a group that *was* different. It triggered the "sense of belonging" that we all crave.

Would it have been just as effective if the call-to-action was "Buy an Apple computer?" No, it wouldn't. It is important to know your audience, their pain points, and what is important to them to create a call-to-action that resonates and creates action.

Don't confuse your audience by having multiple call-to-actions. One website, one action. Don't make your audience work too hard to figure out what to do next. Keep it simple.

CONTENT CAUTIONS

Copyright

ALL PHOTOS, AUDIO, VIDEOS, IMAGES, AND WRITTEN WORKS HAVE COPYRIGHTS. If someone made it, they have the copyright to it unless there is clear permission expressly granted. Do NOT pull stuff from the internet and assume it is fair game. It is illegal to use someone else's work without permission.

In addition to being sued by the creator, social platforms will ding you for copyright infringement or plagiarism and will block your account. It is easy to track an image or written works and see where it is being used through its metadata. Metadata is the information transported and embedded within a file that includes the date it was created, artist, copyright, picture location, and more.

The best way to avoid this problem is to take your own pictures and subscribe to a stock house. Many stock houses offer royalty-free usage. Make sure that you understand their usage agreement. Even within the stock house agreements, there are images that are regulated to editorial (news) use.

NASA has images, audio, and videos that are free to use. These can be found at images.nasa.gov or windowsonearth.org. Check NASA's guidelines for usage at www.nasa.gov/multimedia/guidelines.

Creative Commons is another place to get images. Creators will include their level of permission to use their images. (Note: This is a good spot to give away some of your images that promote your brand.)

Let it go into the world

Done is never perfect. Perfect is never done. – Sheryl Sandberg

Get the content out. Content can be fiddled with until it is stale or dead. Too many times I have watched as good content died because it kept being edited "to get it just right." It is important to make sure the brand is well represented, the grammar is good, keywords are included, and the facts are correct. Let it go into the world, learn what works and doesn't work, and apply it to the next one.

It is like building a rocket engine. The build begins with all of the knowledge you have and then you ignite it to see what happens. Will you know how to make a better engine if the first one is never finished? How many engines will you have to build to get something that is perfect? Same thing with content development, though it is much cheaper to launch.

We can strive to be perfect, but don't sacrifice an opportunity to touch your audience in exchange for a little polish. Get the message where it needs to be, when it needs to be there, and start working on the next one. Learn and repeat.

CHAPTER 10

CONTENT AND SEO

Search Engine Optimization (SEO) is using the tools and knowledge available to make your content more attractive to the search bots and meet the needs of the algorithm in order to push your company up in the search results.

Search engines crawl content with bots to gather information about a website. These bots gather keywords, text, text styles, alternate text, captions, file names, tags, code, download speed, page structure, subtitles, comments, links to and from, popularity, and more. It takes this information and applies an algorithm to it to determine the relevance and compatibility for a search.

Search engines care about their audiences' experience and works very hard to give them exactly what they are searching for in their queries. If they did not do this, we would be overrun with results that were not relevant to our search and our frustration would force us to use another service.

BE FOUND

After we create content, we want it to be found. Content feeds the search engines that will direct them to your website or social platforms. Keywords and terms need to be present on your site for the search engines to bring your company up in the results.

Search engines understand relevance and reward those companies that provide engaging content. Keyword-stuffing (having nothing but keywords in your article for the sole purpose of search) or any other kind of trickery will get you blocked.

DON'T: Do NOT lie, deceive, or use bad grammar. SEO gods don't like it. (I am serious about the grammar part. It will get you dinged.)

DO: Answer the questions people have in easy-to-understand and relevant terms.

Content should pique interest and drive viewers to your website. Once there, content needs to provide answers to the audiences' questions without any friction. Friction, such as gatekeepers that force someone to give an email address, will drive them to another source.

I recently saw a conference post for a space organization. I went to the site to see how much it cost. You had to enter all kinds of information just to get the price. It was buried. I was not willing to give that much information just to see if I could afford to go. In addition to the frustration of not finding what I was looking for, I think less of them for trying to "fleece" me for my information.

Cost is an important consideration when choosing which conferences that I wanted to attend for the year. Not only did they NOT make my list, but they were also blackballed from ALL of my future lists.

A potential customer will typically deeply research a small purchase before they commit. How much more research do you think they will do for a high-dollar item like a payload service?

They will search until they feel informed enough to make a decision, and then reach out to the possible vendors that they TRUST to take care of them. They will select only those vendors that they believe will give them the best value. Is that the company that buried their information at the start of the research cycle? Not usually.

How many companies design their content to confound their competition rather than providing the information that their audience needs?

FINDABILITY VERSUS DISCOVERABILITY

Findability refers to how easy it is for someone to find the information that they are seeking, whereas discoverability is someone finding information that they were not originally looking for in a search. Findability is about the searcher looking for you or your information. It is not about pushing your way into view. As advertisers, we tend to be more aggressive and lazier.

Think of findability as the candy pieces that led ET up to Elliott's home. Findability is a better tactic in this day-in-time when users are shying away from overly aggressive tactics.

There are ways to make pages findable. Content needs to be available using keywords and phrases for subjects that people want to know more about and are relevant to the industry. You can enhance findability by adding keywords to headings, tags, alternate text, captions, and subtitles.

KEYWORDS AND KEYWORD PHRASES

Keywords are words and phrases that people type into search engines to find what they are looking for. Example of a keyword – *"rocket."* A single word could have multiple meanings. Is this a toy rocket? Is this a STEM search? Are the searchers model makers or engineers? Are they looking for SpaceX or Orion launches? These types of results are general.

Keyword phrases are a set of words that narrow down the search. Example "Rocket payload services." You can see that it is more specific than the single word "rocket."

Longtail keyword phrases are referring to phrases that are very specific. The longer the phrase, the more specific the results will be. These people are more intentional in their searches. Can you tell what this person's intent is? *"Rocket payload services for Moon supply delivery."* I hope *Rockets-R-Us* has an article about this on their website.

Even if *Rocket-R-Us* does not have this capability, their content can discuss where they are on the development of it, what kind of rockets are needed to do this type of mission, or who does have this capability.

AUDIENCE SEARCH BEHAVIORS

Who are they and what is their intent with a search? Don't assume that you know. There may be terms that companies think are important, but their audience never think about using them. For example, if I am looking for a used car, would I look for *"previously-owned vehicles"*? Probably not. I would look for *"used cars."* I would refine my search with *"used Tesla in [insert location]."* That will get a more specific result list that shows my intention.

KEYWORD LIST

I recommend developing a list of relevant keywords and keyword phrases to aid search engines in finding your content. There are several tools to provide data for keywords and help determine a site's keyword health. Some of them are paid, and a few tools have free versions. Google Trends and Google Ad Planner are free. Other tools are Ask The Public, Spyfu.com, SEO Rush, and Moz Keyword Explorer. I recommend conducting a search for new tools as there are always new ones coming online as the internet evolves.

Even if you do not have a paid ad campaign planned, these tools can demonstrate which keywords and keyword phrases are working. Having a list makes it easier for you to add them to your content and that makes your content easier to find.

An example of this would be the keyword *"space." "Space"* could mean several things from storage units to office real estate. This is one of the main reasons that the term NewSpace is one word and isn't two words "new space." "New space" has a hard time pulling results that are relevant.

(Note: I am not a fan of the term NewSpace. It has a short shelf life. It will only be new for a certain amount of time. The keyword phrase *"Commercial Space Industry"* is timeless and is easier to find in a search)

By adding the word *"industry,"* to *"space,"* there is more of a chance that the article will be found. The more keywords and keyword phrases found in an article, the better job search engines can do when figuring out the content of your article.

USING KEYWORDS

Once you have a good keyword and keyword phrase list, make sure you include them in places that search engines will look for them. Good places for keywords include:

- **Headlines** – Use keywords in headlines. Be clear and descriptive. Long gone are the days where witty and vague headlines were effective. Make sure your headlines have a headline (H#) style applied. H1 is the main headline and H2, H3, H4 are subheading designations. Search engines will look for these styles.
- **Article content** – Make sure to add keywords in your article where they make the most sense. Don't add them for the sake of adding them. The search engine gods look at things like the amount of time a user spends reading the

article and links to the content from outside sources. They also know how to read and give points for relevance.

- **Captions and alternate text for pictures** – Don't leave these blank. They help search engines determine what it is and will help its ranking results.
- **Names for pictures, downloads, and documents.** If you have an image img-0002.jpg, it does nothing to get found. Change it to space-rocket-blasts-Arizona-Xprize.jpg. This picture's name will help it be found in searches versus the generic name. (Make sure it is what you say it is – lies get dinged by search engine gods)
- **Video** – Make sure keywords are in the video title, description, and captions. To add an extra SEO punch, use video transcripts, closed captions, and subtitles.

WARNING

Search engines focus on providing *real* content for their audience and work hard to eliminate anyone trying to game the system. They care about their audiences' experiences with the platform and want to eliminate anything that will send them to a competitor. These keywords must be used naturally in the content. If the search engine believes the article has been stuffed with keywords, they will ding the content. Make no mistake – search engines can read and it *understands* what it reads.

Keyword-stuffing is considered a black hat tactic. Black hat tactics are considered to be deceptive practices aimed to drive traffic to a dangerous or bogus site. Keyword stuffing is when an article is full of keywords for the sake of having keywords. It lacks readability or any valid information.

GOLDEN SEO RULE

Treat people like you would like to be treated. Produce good content for your audience using appropriate keywords and good grammar. Yes, good grammar counts in SEO ranking.

Search engines rule the world of findability. We need to play their game if we want to pop to the top of their results. They are always looking for ways to make these results more relevant to their search audience and are constantly adding tweaks to the algorithm.

In May of 2021, Google updated its algorithm to include a factor called Page Experience. It prioritizes page load speeds, responsiveness, user experience, mobile usability, and security. Google will look for interaction and looks at things like conversion rates and Call-to-actions.

Google provides many tools and information to help you with SEO. Two places to begin are:
https://search.google.com/test/mobile-friendly
https://developers.google.com/speed/pagespeed/insights/

I recommend reading articles based on these new changes in the algorithms and keep your content relevant if being found is important to your strategies. The more competitive that your space is, the more attention this will require.

CHAPTER 11

TYPES OF CONTENT
EDITORIAL-BASED CONTENT

Editorial-based content is content designed to inform, educate or entertain that is published in print or online. It is not content that attempts to sell something. Content that focuses on selling would be considered an ad, or commercial content.

Editorial-based content provides an opportunity to demonstrate knowledge, experience, and authority. This strategy is critical to establishing your brand's placement as an industry leader. It is also critical that content exists so that your brand can be found.

Select engaging topics that are of interest to your audience. This may be obvious by now, but it bears repeating for clarity. This is determined by what you learned by developing a persona, interviews, and research about who your audience is.

Search engines rely on words to pull searches. Editorial-based content is a must in order to be found. Having the words available online is not enough to pull rank and place at the top of the results. Keywords, links, tags, alternative text, and correct grammar are graded by search engines to like your editorial content and deem it worthy of consideration. It is not all that must be done, but it is a start. People have to like your brand's content as well in order to place it in the coveted top search results.

Please note that this criterion is still relevant even if you throw money at Google, Bing, or Yahoo. You still need to have actual content in existence that people want in order to rank in any search results. No content = nonexistence.

In the Google study by Google/Millward Brown Digital, B2B Path to Purchase Study in 2014, 90% of people use online search specifically to research business purchases. The research also shows that those involved in the buying process are already 57% of the way down the path to a decision before performing an action on a website.

What does this mean to your brand? You need lots of good quality content to inform to have any chance of being found.

Where to have content

Go where your brand's audience is looking. Be in all of the places that your audience is listening, looking, and searching. This includes, but not limited to, publications (on and offline), your brand's website, social media platforms, podcasts, books, videos, serving as conference guest speakers, etc.

NASA is the best example of a content development powerhouse within the space industry, and I suggest looking at what they do. They have been presenting great content that educates and inspires since the early 1960s. They have something in every category that you can imagine.

Types of editorial-based content

Articles

Articles are the base of content and are critical for online and offline awareness. In the online world, it provides the means in order to be found by search engines. Search is how most people find information about ideas, products, services, etc. As an audience is researching a subject, they come across the answers to their questions.

Be the one that supplies the answer.

Articles that answer an audience's question allows them to consume information on their own time, and on their own terms. It builds trust with the entity that supplies these answers and positions the entity as the industry expert. Be that entity.

Blog posts

These are different than regular articles. It has more of a conversational tone and expresses points of view or opinions.

News releases

Press releases were once vital for getting company news to reporters, news outlets, and journalists. It was a critical venue and owned by the media. Press releases were used as only a part of the information that reporters gathered to write their articles. Times have changed.

Nowadays, many publications have reduced their staff and rely heavily on information and ready-to-go articles from other sources, such as your company. The new term is "news releases" because it doesn't rely on the press as the main source of information for news. Many companies now develop their own pipelines to get their news releases into the world.

Tactic: A news release has a particular structure that provides the facts of an event. Take this a step further by constructing an additional article format that is ready for smaller news outlets to copy and paste into their publications as a feature story. They will need a great story from your company along with great pictures and full captions.

Take it another step further by developing videos and social posts to get more reach out of an article.

Whitepapers

These are usually a 12–40-page ebook of complex information that has been reworked for easy consumption with visual elements. Many brands exchange an email for this ebook download so they can send additional information later.

Case study

Case studies provide a story format that can provide easy consumption of a concept and make it applicable to the audience. It can provide inspiration as well as ideas with a "Hey, they did this, so can I!" This type of content demonstrates the challenge, the solution, and the results of a particular example, client, subject, or event.

Publications

These include newsletters, manuals, magazines, or books. Most options for this type of content have an opportunity for online and offline production. Even if the publication is offline, they probably have an online version. These can consist of direct downloads, subscriptions sent via email, or print sent via U.S. postal service.

Make sure that the online version links to your brand's website. This is a key component to search engines deciding on the top placement of search results.

Syndication

Articles can be syndicated to other publications as guest or feature writers. Syndication is having an article ready for publication or broadcast to multiple newspapers, periodicals, websites, stations, etc.

Syndicate or provide your content to other organizations so that it can be published or shown in several places where your audience may be spending time. An example could be a guest writer for a magazine where content such as a feature article is provided on a regular basis. This can be a way to expand your brand's authority and increase awareness with your audience.

SOCIAL MEDIA POSTS

Social media is an important component for your marketing strategies. A healthy following builds over time if they want the content you provide. It is a slow process.

ALERT: If you build a following too fast, your account will be flagged. DO NOT BUY FOLLOWERS! EVER. EVER-EVER! You will get dinged and blacklisted.

The internet search engines and social platforms reward honest behaviors that improve a user's experience and punishes those who try to take shortcuts. Don't do it.

Aim to provide interesting and/or entertaining posts with audience-relevant content.

Requirements

Different platforms have different requirements for posts. Some have daily post limits, video length allowances, character limits for the message, and restrictions for word counts within an image.

There are other legal restrictions like posting images that have a copyright. *(NOTE: ALL images have a copyright.)* Make sure you have permission to use the images in your posts. A platform has the right to close your page for infringement.

Each post should be constructed to be relevant for that platform. For example, LinkedIn posts have a very different feel and conversation than Twitter or Facebook posts. Design content that appeals to the audience of the platform that you are using.

What are your audience's expectations? Are they looking for business trend information on LinkedIn or entertaining conversation that can be found on Twitter?

Note: The exact same content can do well on one platform and bomb on another. Each platform has its own personality and audience expectations. If you have a piece of content that is newsworthy or answers a question, don't write it off if it falls flat on one platform. Try it on several platforms and tweak the information so it appeals to that platform.

Timing

Timing plays a large part in the success of a piece of content. Look for trends and piggyback on other news stories. This is called news-jacking. A series of posts about Mars will do better if it is launched in conjunction with a major event like the Perseverance landing.

Platform Development

Focus on the platforms that you will consistently use and are dedicated to developing. It is a time-intensive activity, and it is a better use of your effort to focus only on developing the platforms that are most relevant to your audience. (Note: It is still recommended that you secure your name on all major social platforms.)

VIDEO

Native posting

Native videos are videos that are directly uploaded to a social platform. These videos rank higher in feeds than images. However, a link to a video that takes a user to another social platform is considered competition and generally does not rank as well.

In a 2019 Statista article, native videos were the top-performing types of content on Facebook and earned the most engagements among top posts. They generated more shares than every other content format.

Determine your goals when deciding on a link or native upload. If your company's YouTube is monetized, it may be worth having a lower reach on Facebook. If the goal is a higher reach on Facebook, then native upload is the way to go.

Size and length: Different platforms have different length and size requirements that can range from six seconds to a max of 12 hours or 128GB (YouTube). Research the chosen platform for their requirements. Some requirements are square, others are vertical or horizontal rectangles. These requirements change often, so check them routinely.

Videos have an ideal length for the most watchability or a sweet spot. Focus on what is best for your message. If a 20-minute video is what your audience needs, don't dumb it down to hit a two minute "optimum" length.

To be or not to be viral

Focus on the goal of what you want to achieve for your audience, not on creating a viral video. Going viral is icing on the cake if it goes in that direction. It is better to have ten videos that have

100,000 views each that contains the right message for your audience than a single viral video that receives one million views from people who are not your target audience.

Production quality

There are many free tools available that can add a professional touch and enhance your video.

- Edit out the parts that don't lends itself to the story. (This is easily done with free software)
- Music and sound effects can be easily added.
- Bumpers (introduction and exit brand animation) can be created from freelance platforms like Fivrr.com for little investment.

Aim to resonate. Some situations may need a high production value such as an animation of a space station. However, other videos may not have to look like a big production. In some instances, if it is too polished, it may come off as a sales commercial that may turn off a lot of viewers. Remember, it is all about *the story* and filling the audience's needs.

Webinar/webcast – Live or on-demand

These types of videos are a great way for connecting with your audience, answer questions, and promote your brand as an expert in its field.

There are opportunities for sponsorship, guest speakers, and demonstrations. Record the webinar and post it in your library for even more engagement from those who want to rewatch it or those people that could not make the time to attend.

According to author Joe Pulizzi, in 2013, 80% of those who signed up for a webinar or webcast attended the live event or watched the recording. That was then. COVID has made an impact in this arena making it more important than ever and we can expect that percentage to grow.

One example that taught me a valuable lesson for the value of recorded webinars was a retirement agency training video. We had set up a campaign for training members about their retirement accounts. The first webinar was full with 40 attendees. We captured and created a video during the presentation then posted it on the company's YouTube account. The second live webinar had nine people registered – nine!.

At first blush, this would indicate that it was a bust. Not true. The YouTube video went on to represent two-thirds of the watch-time for the entire library after a year. Thousands of members watched and rewatched it. What we discovered is that the audience wanted to watch it on their schedule, not ours. Now, it is redone every year with new information, and they don't even bother with the live version.

COVID has made the use of webinars and webcasts more important to any endeavor to get in front of an audience. Social platforms have ramped up their live productions to replace in-person public meetings. Many platforms have initiated new ways to promote these events. This is a trend that bears attention.

VIDEO AND AUDIO PODCASTS

A video or audio podcast is a great way to become established as an industry expert. As commute time increases, audible podcasts are increasing in popularity. Live or recorded video programs are more accessible than ever to a brand.

Having a channel is no longer reserved for the network giants. The equipment needed for production is more cost-effective than ever before and the investment entry-point is attainable for the tightest of budgets. Got a smartphone and a computer?

Podcasts are a great way to hear industry news, interesting interviews, thought-provoking opinions, and to be entertained.

Audiences want a relationship with a likable personality that they can get to know, identify with, and enjoy being around that feeds them information in an interesting and entertaining way.

Podcasts are a great vehicle for promoting your colleagues and customers. Guest speaking and sponsorships provide a value that can strengthen or establish relationships. Making a guest appearance can help a brand get some attention. It can also provide a tool for the hosting brand to encourage new connections. Interested customers can receive an added benefit from the opportunity to present their company to an audience.

That being said, don't have a guest speaker on an episode just for the business value it creates between companies. It needs to resonate with your audience.

Selecting a brand just for the money will reflect badly and threaten the trusting relationship you have developed with your audience. What if their product stinks or doesn't fit the audience's needs? It will make your information less reliable if your audience believes you are for sale to the highest bidder. They will not waste their time with the podcast if they think it is only a sales tool designed to fleece them, yet again.

Program sponsorship can provide income to the podcast while providing valuable exposure to the sponsoring brand. The audience is key for selecting an appropriate sponsor. Always focus on the needs of your audience.

What makes a good podcast?

Book entertaining guests that can speak.

An episode can live for a long time. A mediocre or bad episode can hurt for years. You would not want the first experience someone has with the podcast to be painful. You do not know what episode a listener will start listening to you. More than likely, it won't be at the beginning. They will see something that interests them, and they will begin there. IF they like it, they might go back to the beginning. IF.

Will your audience think the speaker or company is interesting? If the answer is no, move to the next idea for a guest. Your audience is the most important consideration.

Do they have an interesting history or product.? What are their plans for the future? How does what they do connect with your audience?

Can they speak clearly? Listening to mumbling or ums can be irritating, and many listeners will only tolerate so much before they turn off the episode. Once they turn it off, will they come back? Pobably not.

It can be painful to listen to someone that can't speak or answer a question. They need to be able to answer questions clearly with commentary, information, and conversation.

Are they humorous or witty? Audiences like this trait in a speaker. On the other hand, it can be frustrating to listen to speaker who rambles or give answers that are too brief.

A host that is likable.

Make sure your host embodies good speaking traits and won't rub people wrong. They need to have a pleasant voice that can move a conversation into interesting moments. Speaking clearly and with vocal variety is a must for listening pleasure.

Interesting information that entertains.

Develop a plan with subjects and speakers that your audience wants to hear. What does your audience care about? Ask, ask, ask! (I know, I am a broken record about this point) Seek out what is important to them. What inspires, informs, and entertains them? Who are they curious about?

What is your company passionate about? Passion for something is contagious. Even if someone isn't initially interested, a host's passion that is genuine and is represented clearly will get attention. Don't be afraid to show it.

Conversely, if there is no passion for the subject, that will come across as well.

The first episode is the hardest to get off the ground. Once you have momentum, keep going. It is an asset that can lead to other assets in articles, posts, and other marketing ventures. Expand the content to other venues and platforms.

Monetization opportunities for podcasting

Podcasts allow for many opportunities to produce an income. Here are a few ideas.

- Allow YouTube and other platforms to show commercials
- Episode sponsorships
- Sell your products or services (be careful not to be a commercial – this should be a small percentage of the content and should not be the focus of the show)
- Sell guest speakers' products and services as an affiliate (need to be disclosed to the audience by law, and again audience interests should come first)
- Syndication – Sell podcast to different outlets.
- Charge your guest speakers (This option is for podcasts that have a competition for appearances and after some history is developed. Don't let this override your audiences' experiences.)

DEVELOPING CONTENT SUBJECT IDEAS

What kind of content do you create? Here are some ideas for developing content.

- **Answers to questions from customers/potential customers/audience** – Make a list of questions from your interviews from existing customers, leads that didn't convert to a customer, potential customers, and any other audience type that impacts your business.
- **Events** – Promote an event like a rocket testing event or a conference. Even small occasions can be expanded into something remarkable.
  - o **Create an event** - Starting a competition or appreciation banquet can provide news for the brand and the industry.
  - o **Events within your company** - List all of the small and large events.
  - o **Events within the industry** – Highlight and piggyback onto industry news such as the 50th Anniversary of the Moon landing
- **Milestones** - How can milestones be celebrated? Can they be themes for content? Can it become an event that generates excitement?
- **Interesting subjects** - Are you using new technology or a new technique?
  Kentucky Transportation Cabinet started using drones to gather data for building roads and bridge inspections. During a vehicle crash on one of the bridges, the drones provided a valuable contribution to the inspection team. Drone stories and social media posts generated positive feedback during a challenging time.
- **Educational content** – Create content for your audience to learn about the industry, building processes, or business methods. Create a STEM outreach for youth.

- **Interesting facts and figures** – These concepts can be developed into infographics, social posts, articles, videos, and more.
- **Current events** - Look at the current news in the industry. See what is trending in search engines. Newsjacking is when you write about something that is hot in the news. This can be picked up by search engines and highlighted in news feeds. Write about any links that your company has to the news event.
- **Industry trends and concerns** - Make a list of things that are going on in your industry. What are the new trends and what are the concerns that have everyone talking and searching about?
- **Top ten lists** - Articles with important lists do well. Make sure they are easy to consume with things like bullet points.
- **Employee, customer, or audience highlights** - Interviews with your current customers and vendors, initiatives such as minority or gender inclusion, employee morale, job opportunities, and STEM or volunteer outreach can provide interesting content.

Need more content?

Encourage your audience to provide videos, images, and articles. Share content from other business customers, vendors, suppliers, business partners, industry influencers, and your community and/or enlist them to produce content that you can use.

CHAPTER 12

CONTENT PLATFORMS
SOCIAL MEDIA
Respect the platform
Each social media platform has its own personality of followers. One post slammed out to all the social media platforms demonstrates a lack of interest and caring. Each platform has special characteristics and a flavor all its own.

For example, Instagram users have different expectations than Twitter users. *Even if they are the same person, they will expect different things.* Create a plan for each platform to maximize what makes them special. Develop content tailored to the platform that informs and entertains.

Social Platforms
When we think of social platforms, we tend to think of the major players - Facebook, Twitter, Instagram, and LinkedIn. There are several others that may not be as obvious but should not be overlooked.

YouTube is a social platform as well as a powerful search engine. It is owned by Google and video results are promoted more than other findings on search queries.

There are platforms that focus on imagery such as Flikr and Creative Commons. Placing pictures on these sites will promote your brand and provide vehicles for people to share your story.

Forum-based discussion groups like Reddit and Quora provide a great place to gather questions and answer a few to establish your brand as the expert.

There are review-based platforms such as Glassdoor and Yelp. Google My Business is another social platform that provides communication with your audience.

SnapChat, Pinterest, Tumblr, Tic Toc, Medium, and the list grows. New platforms like Clubhouse grow while others like Google + die away.

The important thing is to consider where your audience is and what your company can manage effectively.

CHAPTER 13

PLATFORMS

Website

One of the most important content platforms is your website. This is where people will go to find information about your brand, your company, and your industry. Make sure they find it.

Websites are no longer something that is built and forgotten about. Keep it fresh with new information so that people will refer to it often as a source of information.

NASA is a great example of the power of a website, or should I say websites. It is brimming with news and has extensive archives that establish them as experts. They have more pictures, videos, and articles than can be comprehended. It is a bottomless repository of information, tools, and entertainment.

Your website houses information about your organization. It is recommended that an audit of the site's link health be routinely conducted. This ensures that the site is being indexed properly for search engines and that visitors are not experiencing 404 errors.

There are several reporting tools that are available and more coming online every day. Some tools include W3C Link Checker, Site Liner, SEO Quake, SEO Rush, and plain ol' Google search results. Link information can affect how a website will rank. These tools report information for links that are internal, external, broken, orphaned, conical redirections, and unfinished pages. Additional information that is included is duplicated content and backlinks.

All of these issues can impact a search engine's results when people are looking for information that could point them to your website.

Eliminate friction

Friction. The force that slows down momentum. Is it present in your process to be heard and understood? Are you standing in the way of your audience? Are you slowing down the consumption of your information because you want to grab a web visitor's email or is your product a secret? People are tired. Make it easy for them to consume your information.

Plus, most of us are very limited on time. We don't have the energy nor the time to figure out your secret. We are going to someone who can give us the answers we need...now. This instant. Not with a phone call where someone can "sell" us.

"But, we want them to call so we can explain it to them." Here is the reality. By the time someone does make the call, the decision has already been made. They have received the majority of the information that they needed in order to convince their boss and initiate action. Did you give them what they needed or did your competition?

What does your audience really want to know? GIVE IT TO THEM OR THEY WILL FIND ANOTHER SOURCE. You want your brand to be the expert and the source of their answers.

"But, my competition will know my price, service, and information!" So will your customer. Who will make you more successful? If you fail to provide the information that they are searching for, restrict it, or make it difficult to find, your *potential* customer will be forced to get it somewhere else... probably your competition.

Test your user's experience through your website and your sales process. Eliminate any friction that you may find. Focus on providing a positive and informative experience. It will be worth the effort.

CHAPTER 14

NEW TECHNOLOGIES

There are new technologies being developed every day and they will affect marketing in the future. As COVID changes the landscape, new technologies will roll out and provide new opportunities for marketing. The technologies in this section will impact marketing in ways that may be unexpected.

Virtual Reality (VR) is where a user enters a new reality when they put on goggles. The real world disappears and is replaced with an alternate experience. With Augmented Reality (AR), a user can see what is surrounding them and digital information is overlayed on top of the real world. Mixed Reality (MR or XR) combines a blend of the physical and digital worlds. MR goggles can "see" what is around the user through its eye and hand tracking components which adds to the experience. MR combines immersive computer-generated environments with real physical elements. This provides users with tactile muscle memory that is valuable with training.

AUGMENTED REALITY

Augmented Reality (AR) is here and making itself known. You already have the capability on your smartphone. Many industries are using it to try on products, pick furniture for your house, or play games like Pokémon Go. It has been used in several industries for years prior to the current adoption of the mainstream public.

It is already being used in aerospace and defense to design products such as engines. Some companies simulate dangerous training scenarios in this safe environment. It is also used to work to optimize assembly lines, monitor or repair systems, and train employees.

STEM Outreach

There are multiple apps available for tablets and phones that bring space to the masses. One example of an app produced by NASA's Jet Propulsion Laboratory displays 3D spacecraft models to users. Spacecraft AR displays spacecraft such as the Curiosity Mars rover into any environment with a flat surface with no target (printed paper) required. It displays mission information and has a function that allows the user to see the craft at full size.

Another app called SkyView lets users point their device (phone or tablet) upward and see what star or planet is in the night sky.

NASA has implemented AR technology in journals and notebooks that are aimed at all ages to excite youth about space. Immersive experience generates excitement more effectively than reading about it or watching a video.

Manufacturing

AR is utilized for the Artemis program to the Moon. Lockheed Martin began using AR in 2017 to increase efficiency in building the spacecraft for the Artemis II mission. Instead of getting detailed work procedures from a book or models on a 2-D screen, the instructions are visually overlaid in 3-dimensional space onto the real spacecraft using AR goggles. This provides quicker understanding and aids in assembling complex hardware that requires multiple teams. Things that used to take a week can be done in one shift.

Repair

Airplane mechanics are using AR to streamline a time-consuming process of consulting maintenance manuals. GE Aviation mechanics use AR goggles to pinpoint issues and assist with repair. Goggles retrieve information about what you are looking at and overlay images that provide invaluable directions. This can have a large impact on business operations.

For example, a technician can be looking at a motor that needs repairs. If it is a model that they have not seen before, they can have another technician walk them through the repair from a completely different location. Both technicians can see the engine. Directions are overlayed and pointers assist the hands-on repair saving valuable time in research, cost, and adding to the level of competence in completing the job.

VIRTUAL REALITY

Virtual Reality (VR) is an immersive experience in another world or dimension. It uses goggles that transport a user into a digital world. This world can be 100% fabricated, use real-life replications, or a combination of the two. Generally, people think of gaming when VR is discussed. However, it is a valuable tool for designing and simulating inventions, complex systems, and processes.

Virtual reality has been used for a while to design and simulate things in the aerospace and defense world. One example is Embraer. This aircraft company has used VR since February 2000. They use this technology to gain greater precision in their systems analysis. They set up a VR operation in São Paulo to aid in the development process of the EMBRAER 170/190 commercial aircraft. VR shortened the time it took to complete the design of the jet from a 60-month process down to 38 months.

NASA has utilized this technology since 2016 for science. They have discovered new information about stars and how they work. VR has virtual hands-on applications for engineers working on satellite servicing missions and next-generation space exploration.

Training

How can this technology be used for marketing? Training is one of the valuable aspects of this technology. Education and training are powerful forms of marketing. Imagine a student being trained to work on a specific engine for a specific company. Will that student have dedication to that company and its culture? Will decision-makers gravitate towards a solution that safely and effectively trains its users?

The International Air Transport Association (IATA) uses VR to train ground crew and flight attendants. Training time is shorter, and elements are more embedded in the memory as employees can conduct flight checks as they virtually walk around an aircraft, detect any issues, and check safety equipment.

Situations can be created that are rarely experienced but can be destructive if they come to pass. In the virtual world, scenarios can be created that test the employees and prepare them for emergency or unexpected situations that can occur in reality. It can save many lives if the crew have experience in these situations.

New technology requires expert care and maintenance. Technicians can get vital experience in a virtual environment before the new equipment arrives. NASA is using VR to train astronauts for spacewalks. Boeing trains astronauts for flights on the Starliner using VR/MR to pilot the spacecraft to the ISS.

The training can be done remotely. The other astronauts in the team can train together from different locations. This allows an international component where astronauts from other countries can easily train together.

Generate excitement

This technology is only waiting for the limitations of the hardware to catch up to be fully adopted by the mainstream public. The biggest hurdle for mainstream adoption will be eliminated when 5G capabilities are available. The technology is rumbling like a rocket preparing to escape gravity. It is closer than you may think.

This technology can be used to get people excited about space by letting them experience it in an intimate way. Having intimate exposure with your brand will affect how those users interact with your brand in the future. When NASA's New Horizons spacecraft flew past Pluto and its moons, it scanned the planet and provided loads of data. The New York Times worked with the Lunar and

Planetary Institute and the Universities Space Research Association to create a virtual world that was available using Google Cardboard. This provided an experience for the public to examine this tiny planet (it is still a planet for me, so let's not go there) and be inspired by the new information.

NASA uses this technology to provide amazing experiences to increase STEM interest and market the space industry. There are experiences for walking on the Moon, visiting the International Space Station, and participating in prelaunch activities on the Orion Spacecraft.

I was able to walk on the Moon when VR first began projecting via the smartphone ten years ago. The technology was... well... less than stellar at the time. Recent advances have made this a viable option.

Conduct business

There will be a need for VR as COVID lingers and changes how business can be done. COVID has pushed the adoption a little closer to everyday life, but it is not new to business operations.

Disney Imagineers have worked in the virtual space to build theme parks and test it before the first brick is laid in construction. Designers collaborated from around the world and brought skills together without physical relocation.

VR provides human interaction and collaboration from those working remotely. As the technology improves and becomes more mainstream, having a VR conference capability could provide a more personal touch with potential customers and investors. Keep an eye on this tool as when it is adopted by the mainstream public, it will change things as swiftly as the iPhone.

NASA is definitely taking it seriously. NASA is using this technology to implement cross-collaboration between their communication networks. Engineers and scientists will be able to fully interact with the visualization.

NASA is working on intra-agency virtual reality meetups for cost-saving design reviews and using VR for mission support. NASA's Restore-L project is developing tools, technologies, and techniques needed to extend the lifespans of satellites, the Wide Field Infrared Survey Telescope (WFIRST) mission, and various planetary science projects.

NASA's VR/AR team created a framework called the Mixed Reality Engineering Toolkit and is training groups on how to work with it. This new technology helps with science-data analysis and enables VR-based engineering design. It is used for building concept designs for CubeSats to simulate hardware integration, testing for missions, and in-orbit visualizations. (Contact NASA if you are interested in learning more)

APPLY IT

Education and training are big marketing strategies. This is the core of NASA's outreach programs. *What training works with a virtual world?* In the *Rockets-R-Us* example, they might use this technique to train people how to work on, or build, rocket engines or satellites.

Rockets-R-Us has opted to use training strategies for future customer engagement earlier in the journey for the satellite business. One series involve VR as a platform. The VR training that they developed allows potential customers to interact with the different components of a satellite to see what options can benefit their company. They can add or take away functions on the satellite to see what happens in orbit and interact with other considerations or possible ideas they had not considered.

The VR experience allows them to take a ride to the different levels of orbits in different size rockets to see how it relates to the satellite's capabilities and options. This immersive experience is both educational and entertaining as they virtually fly around the Earth.

This virtual experience could stimulate a different need for a more powerful rocket that reaches a different orbit resulting in a larger purchase from the client. People are more likely to reach higher when they know why they should.

This same virtual experience can be used in schools to educate and inspire the next generation. This experience will establish a relationship with their *Rockets-R-Us* brand. It could inspire young adults to choose a satellite career. These choices impact future launch buyers as well as future employees for the company. In addition, this outlet provides opportunities for many conversations through articles, videos, social posts, etc.

Education builds trust. When it comes time to pick a launch vehicle, those companies that already know *Rocket-R-Us* will have a relationship established with them through the training. When spending thousands to millions of dollars, people will pick those companies that they know and trust over the lowest bidder.

Another marketing strategy could be product placement in someone else's VR experience. This can be useful from either side of the partnership. A vendor or strategic partner could pay to be a part of the *Rockets-R-Us* VR experience thus help cover the cost of development. For *Rockets-R-Us*, this could be a satellite component manufacturer. The satellite used in the VR experience would sport the satellite's company logo. *Rockets-R-Us* could sponsor a part in someone else's VR experience as the rocket that lifts off towards the sky with their logo emblazoned on the hull for an emotional moment that connects their brand to the audience.

Note: Put some time and thought into your brand's image beyond just the logo. One of my favorite rocket body designs is Firefly Aerospace. I can see that rocket hurtling to space as part of a VR or movie experience.

BLOCKCHAIN

The internet provides the world that we live in. Blockchain impacts this world and will be bigger in the future. What is blockchain? In layman's terms, it is code that makes something unique. Its code makes it unduplicatable in the digital world. Blockchain is how bitcoin works. This enables things to be sold and traded. Think of it as a real Ming vase versus a picture of one. The real thing has value and is unique. Blockchain enables digital assets like money, art, and even clothing to remain one-of-a-kind items within the online world.

Blockchains are used in banking, supply chains, token-based reward programs, real estate transactions, anything that relies on something to stay authentic and unduplicated.

Good marketing provides value to an audience. Blockchain is a tool that can create value and draw an audience.

This technology can be vital in the collection and sales of data, supply chain, and similar business operations. Boeing is using this technology integrating an IoT-driven (IoT references the Internet of Things) blockchain into their engineering operations by tracking hundreds of thousands of components that it takes to build an aircraft.

A great example of how a company is using this technology for marketing purposes is Gucci. Gucci has used this technology to sell virtual sneakers. Yes - sell sneakers at $9-12 a pop that you cannot wear in real life. Buyers use AR technology to take pictures of themselves wearing them. These AR sneakers are linked to a blockchain-based certificate of ownership called non-fungible tokens (NFTs). Unlike other blockchain products, this sneaker cannot be resold to anyone else.

This prompts the desire to purchase of real one for a much higher price and places the brand as an elite fashion accessory. This was a wise play for a fashion product during the COVID period where fashions were not getting the normal exposure.

CHAPTER 15

ANALYTICS

Why are analytics important? After a company begins to build their goals, they need to know if their activities are working. Analytics establishes a base before the goals are implemented, monitor milestones of the goal, and provide data to determine when success has been reached.

A project begins by creating goals along with key performance indicators (KPI) to monitor progress. Some basic analytics can be established to keep an eye on the successfulness of the goals.

One metric does not complete the story. It is a group of metrics that provide a more comprehensive picture of what is happening.

Analytics is one of the easier things to measure. Google Analytics and social platforms offer it freely as a part of a business account. However, analytics are not the only KPIs that should be measured. Leads, sales, costs, and profits are also examples of KPIs that determine the success of a goal and objective. A great book that digs deeper into this subject is *Measure What Matters* by John Doerr.

Google Analytics is a free tool to measure things such as the amount of website traffic, where the visitors came from, how long they stayed, what they did while they were on the site, and when they left.

Note: Google Analytics does not begin measuring data until an account is established. Each day is processed based on the requested information. It cannot go back and recapture data it was not tasked to monitor.

Rockets-R-Us example

Rockets-R-Us has posted a series of new articles about a bundle program they have developed. The articles were not getting the average traffic activities that their other articles received. They noted that people were landing and immediately leaving the pages. This is called a bounce and can indicate that the search results were not giving visitors what they were looking for in their search.

Rockets-R-Us re-evaluated their keywords usage in their articles. They researched what terms their audience were using for their search queries. They utilized reports from online tools and their usability studies to fine-tune their keyword lists. They discovered that there were some terms that they had not thought about and some longtail phrases that could be added to clarify the message. They rewrote the articles to include these keyword findings.

Traffic responses to the changes were successful. Visitors spent more time on the page indicating that they were reading the article. More importantly, they traveled to other pages within the site. Subscriptions to the newsletter increased and there was an increase in leads that inquired about the program.

Tools that were used in this example were Google Analytics, Google Search Console, Google Keyword Planner, and they conducted user experience studies with a target group of people.

Analytics can be monitored to the minutest of detail and down to the moment an activity occurs. An entire team and thousands of dollars can be devoted to it. However, there are free tools from Google and social media platforms that are very effective to monitor how content is doing and help provide information for formulating more content.

There are many options available to help monitor online activities. Some paid services can integrate offline activities. The range for services can go from free to thousands of dollars per month. The following are some basic metrics to consider that are free options and what they show.

METRICS
Social media metrics

Social media accounts have basic analytics available through their respective platforms that are free. There are some paid social media management systems available that will help consolidate the analytics across multiple platforms. Determine what metrics are important to the strategy that is being monitored. Here are some common metrics:

1. **Engagement metrics such as Shares and Likes** – You can have a million followers but if there are two shares, it didn't do well.
2. **Comments** - Is the post generating conversation? This includes the types of comments such as positive or negative and the content of the comments. What are they saying and why are they saying it? This can impact the content that gets developed in the future and provides a valuable avenue for conversation.
3. **Reach metrics** - This demonstrates how well content worked with the algorithms and the size of the potential audience.
4. **Followers** - This number is important because it represents the potential of the audience size. This does not mean that the entire follower group will see your content. If a piece of content does not generate interest right away, the content can be pushed down the feed or not show at all even to those that follow your feed.
5. **Mentions** - Mentions are online references to your company, brand, or services. This shows who is talking

about you. They occur in product or service reviews, blog posts, educational content, and news articles. Analyze the type of mentions in addition to where it originated.

6. **Video view time** – Average viewing time can show how long the video was viewed. YouTube analytics can show where the viewers left. This can aid with learning what works and what doesn't.

Website metrics

Google Analytics is a wealth of information about the activity that happens on your website. The following are some useful metrics that can help monitor activity for content.

1. **Traffic** – How many visits have there been to the piece of content? This determines if there is a desire to see this type of content. It measures the popularity of the information. Create specific landing pages for campaigns to help isolate what is working within a campaign.
2. **Absolute unique visitors-** This metric shows how many people visit the website. It is a more relevant metric that provides a truer number than the Unique Visitors metric.
3. **Page Visits** - Show which pages visitors are going so it can be determined which pages are relevant. This allows for new content to be developed that provides the information that people are looking to find.
4. **Referral source** – Where was the traffic from? This determines if it is coming from search, email campaigns, other pages on the website, other websites that linked to your website, or social media activities.
5. **Time on page** – How long did visitors spend with the piece of content? It takes a certain amount of time to read or look at the content. This measures the level of engagement with the information.
6. **Bounce rate** – Did the visitors see the page and bounce away? This would indicate that the promised content was not delivered, and the keywords may need adjusting. It

could also represent a problem with the page or code. One of my clients redid their website and updated it to use a more current version of SharePoint. The bounce rate went from 50% to less than 1% overnight due to a change in the coding.

7. **Behavior flow** – Where did the visitors go after they spent time with the piece of content? This would demonstrate that they found the content useful and interesting. It would show if they went on to other pages and which pages prompted them to travel deeper into the site. It would demonstrate the effectiveness of the call-to-action that was on the page. This report also shows where they left the site.

8. **Goal Conversion** – This metric helps determine how many visitors completed a desired action. This could include the use of a free tool, listen to a podcast, download a guide, read a report, sign up for a subscription, make a call, or register for a free trial.

Email metrics

Email strategies can be great tools. There are several email clients available that will help monitor activities resulting from your email strategies. "Email clients" are email services such as MailChimp or HubSpot. Metrics can include:

1. **Open rate** – This shows how many people opened their email and how many times they opened it. This metric only counts the open if the images are downloaded. If they have image blockers and open the email, it will not count.

2. **Click through** – This metric shows you how many people on your list are engaging with your content. It shows what links they clicked on within the email.

3. **Bounce** – This is important because it shows how many people did not receive the email. Soft bounces are the result of a temporary problem with a valid email address, such as a full inbox or a problem with the recipient's

server. Hard bounces are the result of an invalid, closed, non-existent, or suppressed email address. Suppressed results can be addresses where the subscriber opted-out. A hard bounce can be caused by incorrectly entered emails that have misspellings. Hard bounce addresses need to be removed because internet service providers (ISPs) use bounce rates as one of the key factors to determine an email sender's validity.

4. **Unsubscribe Rate** – The CAN-SPAM ACT is the law where you are required to remove someone from your mailing list after they request removal or you can be fined by the Federal Trade Commission $43,792 PER EMAIL that you send them after a 10-day period. This is the main reason I am a fan of email clients because they provide this service, and it does not need to be done manually.

Income

The bottom line - At the end of the day, this is the metric that means the most. Is the content increasing sales or bringing in income? This can be a difficult thing to measure for each individual campaign. There are tools that can measure how many times a person has seen some of the content.

Many marketing campaigns can be monetized and bring in an income. For example, if you have enough subscribers, YouTube videos can be monetized. Ask the question – Is there a way to make money from this marketing direction?

Analytic conclusion

In conclusion, figure out early in the process what metrics your company needs to track and gather the numbers before beginning any new strategies.

PART 2

SPACE MARKETING STRATEGIES

Businesses struggle to adapt to the altering landscape of marketing and are quick to jump onto the latest bandwagon that promises success. Unfortunately, many of the strategies that are out there provide quick fixes that may work for a moment then will fade away like a bottle rocket. The simple secret to successful marketing is having a relationship with your audience. Focus on those tools that can provide that connection.

Everything your brand does matters. And everything is marketing. Marketing is how the world sees your brand.

These successful strategies revolve around building a relationship with your market. It is not about a quick sale. It takes a long viewpoint mixed with time and effort.

CHAPTER 16

EVENTS

NEWSWORTHY EVENTS

The world watched as Neil Armstrong took the first step on the Moon and spoke the legendary words, "That's one step for Man, one giant leap for mankind." This moment did not happen by accident. It could have happened without the cameras and almost did. There was discussion against having the eyes of the world watching every moment of this journey. "What if something goes wrong" some would say. Thankfully, the nay-sayers did not win. That single moment changed lives and inspired the dreams of several generations.

Make your news

Sir Richard Branson, Virgin's iconic CEO, has been successful at making his own news for the publicity, branding, and a little adventure for decades. He looked at opportunities to break world records. He selected those record-breaking events that would align with the company and put the Virgin brand in the spotlight and in the newspapers.

Virgin Atlantic was a new airline that was competing against British Airways. He *could have* bought ads in newspapers and television just like everyone else. But he chose to invest his money in something that would make an impact and put his airline "on the map." By investing his money in a big event instead of traditional ad spending, he could maximize his budget while creating a brand personality that embodied fun and adventure. It would have to match his brand and catch the attention of the public and the media. He decided to break world records.

Branson has broken seven world records. Some of the most notable records were: In 1986, he drove the Virgin Atlantic Challenger II powerboat achieving the fastest Atlantic crossing; In 1987, he was the first to fly a hot air balloon to cross the Atlantic and then again in 1991 across the Pacific; In 2005, he piloted the Virgin Atlantic GlobalFlyer aircraft as it flew a solo nonstop flight around the world.

All of these crafts were sporting the Virgin name as he made the news. They promoted the brand. The spirit of the events embodied flight and speed. The red Virgin brand was prominent on everything.

Another point is that he did not do it alone. All of his events, past and current, usually have multiple partners. Other brands shared in the glory and the expense. This allows the event to be bigger and more spectacular. Each partner has their own large audiences, so the event is promoted exponentially.

CAUTION

Be careful with relying on the prime attention span of the public. As we enter into new areas of discovery and achievements, conquering space is newsworthy. These events can turn routine as time moves on.

It is a beautiful and moving experience to watch a rocket launch. The first time is glorious, and all eyes are on the event. But people become complacent and desensitized even to something as grand as a launch. A good example of this desensitization is the Space Shuttle program. The first few launches were widely viewed with a high pitch of excitement. Then the launches became commonplace. After a few years, the majority of the public only paid attention when would have a catastrophic event.

APPLY IT

- What events can you use to build your brand?
- What kind of event can you create that has impact?
- How can your company get the biggest bang with a limited amount of money?
- What brand partners could you include in the event? List all of the brands that make sense. This can include companies outside of the space industry.
- Note: Make sure you understand the personality of your brand. Be very deliberate in choosing what emotions it embodies. The Virgin brand embodies fun, adventure, and reaching for excellence. His record-breaking events fit the Virgin Airlines brand story with speed and flight.

Celebrate your people

A company is its people. Celebrate your employees and their achievements. People love to hear stories about other people and what they do. A good human-interest story has immense power.

Celebration of your employees does several things The company has content to build its brand, the employees get a pat on the back, and the news outlets get good stories.

By focusing on the wonderful things that your employees do at work and outside of work, it makes for a great moral-booster. It can make the employees feel important and special which increases production and work satisfaction. It spurs other employees to shine.

Celebrating your employees humanizes the company and builds a relationship. People connect with other people. The need for connection inspires decisions that feed the pipeline for future talent. It establishes the brand culture of your company as a place to work and be fulfilled. People may take a position with a company that celebrates their value over another that may pay higher but does not appreciate their workforce.

Human stories provide content that shows the personality of the company. Local papers love to "print" stories about local citizens. Everyone loves to hear a good story.

Make lemonade

Sir Richard Branson is the king of lemonade. He artfully takes any situation and makes it bend in his favor. He looks at the situation and decides to have fun with it. He takes a failure and makes it shine.

In 2013, he lost a bet with Air Asia chief executive Tony Fernandes. The loser had to serve drinks on the winner's airline. It could have been a non-newsworthy event that would pass away in the minds of a few friends. Branson took this negative and had fun with it... very publicly. He dressed as a female flight attendant complete with bright red lipstick and a skirt.

He made it news! Both airlines benefited from this escapade with news coverage. He took other failures such as capsizing Challenger I on his first try to break the TransAtlantic record and the hot-air balloon crash then turned them into positive branding for his companies.

The average person might take these failures, go home to lick their wounds, and never try again. Sir Richard demonstrates that every event, good or bad, can be celebrated. This lemon event can be used to bring out the best in us. His failures make him more relatable and likeable. When he gets knocked down, he picks himself up, and smiles. The story inspires us to do the same. That feeling rubs off on the brand and trickles down the corporate chain.

APPLY IT

- How does your company handle failures?
- How can you turn any situation into a positive story?
- Virgin's personality revolves around fun and adventure in a classy way. Select the words that will describe the personality of your company. Use them to define and measure the company's activities. For example – How can we have fun with this situation? Can we celebrate it?
- How do we demonstrate our ability to pick ourselves up?
- How does this situation relate to what our audience experiences?
- Can this situation become something that inspires our audience?

Toot your horn

If you have a horn, blow it!

It is surprising how little companies celebrate their events, milestones, or people with a press release, a post, or any promotional activity. Some companies are so bogged down with the day-to-day activities that moments of potential celebration pass by without any notice. Sad. What a waste.

This problem is a dangerous mindset issue. This plodding mindset misses the beauty of the journey. It is a view that promotion and public affairs are unimportant or not worth the effort. Compounded with the mistaken expectation that if it is great, the news will notice. Make the media notice your news.

It is easy to fall into the plodding mindset trap. You put your nose to the grindstone and dedicate all of your energy to do something very hard. It's a valiant work ethic, but it can hurt your company if you don't celebrate the steps along the journey.

This dangerous mindset has a domino effect. It says that your employees and their effort lack value. This breeds dissatisfaction.

The more dissatisfaction your team experiences, the more their productivity drops. Why? It proves that nothing they do matters.

Celebrating the milestones is a celebration of the efforts of those who work for you. Employees get re-energized and feel like they are making a difference. Happy employees work better and produce more. Those happy employees are more likely to make your customers happy.

People help people they like. Companies that win usually do not do it alone. They have valuable support in their audience, fans, employees, and colleagues. By celebrating the wins, the company builds a likable personality.

Remember that your brand is like a person. It becomes something that people want to hang around and they become dedicated in helping it succeed. We love to see that pop of success like a firework display as it dazzles us. This tribute draws us in, and we want to be touched by its glory.

Get known

People can't give your company opportunities if they don't know it exists. Promotion is vital to building awareness around your company's brand. Public affairs, marketing, outreach, and promotion need to be a priority in the business of doing business. If it isn't, your brand is like an invisible person with their mouth taped shut.

Maximize those moments.

How can this moment, celebration, or milestone become more - more newsworthy, more interesting, more dazzling, more delightful?

Adding delight

Adding delight is about providing more than what your audience expects. Delighting your audience establishes an emotional bond between them and your brand that is strong.

While the world watched the maiden flight of SpaceX's Falcon Heavy rocket in February 2018, the payload doors opened to reveal a cherry red Tesla car in its cargo bay. The Tesla rocket launch event was layered with delight with details that spoke to the audience. It could have been a blip in the news. But with a little creativity, the event grew and is relevant today as Starman swings past Mars and enters into pop culture.

Sir Branson added delight to the would-be astronauts on the waiting list by adding special VIP benefits. Delight can change the emotion from frustration to extreme happiness.

Delights can be small and powerful. It takes asking the questions, "What would delight my audience?" "What would be unexpected that would make my audience feel important?"

What event can you build and what delights can you add to it?

APPLY IT

- What small and large events does your company have coming up?
- Can they be combined with another event, product, or partner in a unique way?
- What can you add that is unexpected and delightful?
- How can you expand the story?
- How can these events be modified to be something bigger?
- How can you elevate a celebration?
- Do you have a person in place that is focused on promoting the company and its events and milestones?

CREATE AN EXPERIENCE THAT DELIGHTS

One of my favorite techniques is creating something special from things that we already have at our disposal. Or better yet, creating a new marketing event or product from thin air.

Creating an event is a type of vehicle that works well for this tactic. Done correctly, it can forge a powerful connection from the company to their audience making them feel special and included. One of the most powerful emotional connections you can make with an audience is the sense of belonging to a tribe. Building the right event can bring the tribe together like a bonfire.

A sense of belonging creates a strong loyalty and bonds your audience to the company.

Years ago, Pan Am used this marketing technique. The airline invented the First Moon Flights Club during the Apollo moon trips. This was a something-from-nothing marketing tactic designed to promote the reservation feature for the airline. Pan Am issued 93,000 reservation cards to the moon between 1968 and 1971.

Virgin Galactic adopted this strategy in a fabulous way beginning in 2004. They positioned themselves as the world's first commercial spaceline. Unlike Pan Am's free reservation, these tickets to orbit were a hefty $200,000 each.

The first round enlisted 600 people from 58 countries who put down a deposit for a 90-minute flight priced at $200,000. This deposit amount was increased to $250,000 in 2013.

They had ambitious goals of transporting the first tourists by 2007, but a few years turned into almost two decades. This would be a disaster of epic proportions for most companies. Not for the lemonade king. He understands the importance of the tribe and how vital it is to delight his audience.

Virgin Galactic demonstrates the value of respecting your audience. The building of the Spaceship had an ambitious timeline. Virgin Galactic sold tickets to fly to space on a craft that wasn't even cleared to fly commercial passengers or "future astronauts."

As the timeline for the promised passenger flight slipped further into the distant future, Virgin Galactic created a VIP program for the ticket holders. By designing exclusive and unique events, the company formed a fellowship and a value beyond the elusive flight.

True to Sir Branson's and Virgin's reputation, it focused on creating a unique experience and captured a sense of belonging.

Many ticket holders found this experience to be of a greater value than the Spaceship flight.

VIP events included things such as excursions at Sir Richard's island in the Caribbean, a solar eclipse festival in Idaho, test-flight viewings at the Mojave Desert facility, spaceship-shaped cufflinks at Christmas, and campfires at an African game reserve.

Some of these events used established assets such as Sir Richard himself and included outings at his home such as tennis matches, fun lunches, or campfire discussions about the future of space.

Other events were provided by Virgin Galactic's sponsors such as Land Rover. This transfers some of the cost while providing an opportunity for brand supporters to share in delighting the tribe.

The amazing experience of spaceflight is the reason Virgin Galactic exists. Why wait to delight the tribe? Delight can happen all throughout the customer's experience ... and it should. Emotions associated with your brand experience matter. When you build multiple moments of delight over time, it places a business apart from its competition. Those brands that only do the minimum to make a sale are missing a powerful strategy that builds loyalty, fans, and a tribe.

This delighting strategy is a win-win-win for everyone involved. Virgin Galactic received $80 million in deposit income from the tickets that help the program continue and promote its future space services. The ticket holders receive an incredible experience, and the sponsors of those experiences gain exposure and affiliation to an exclusive crowd.

They are getting closer to the reality of commercial spaceflight. Virgin Galactic had a successful test flight to space in December 2018, a passenger test flight in February 2019, and Sir Richard flew in the summer of 2021. This marked the official beginning of space tourism for the company.

How many companies would have suffered a black eye from failing to deliver a promised product or service? Compound this failure with a high price tag and it would have been devastating for most businesses. The usual scenario would have included lawsuits and a ton of bad press. Virgin Galactic asked how they could make their loyal customers happy and they did it.

APPLY IT

- How can you provide an exclusive experience for your customers?
- How can you delight and surprise your loyal fans, audience, and customers?
- What extra step can you take to ensure that your customers' experience goes beyond what is expected?

CREATE AN EVENT

An event can generate buzz for a company or brand. It gives a reason for content to be created and consumed. There is a myriad of reasons that can stimulate an event. If there isn't a good reason, make one up. Here are a few ideas.

- An important milestone celebration –15th launch, 5-10-20+ year anniversary
- Product unveiling – new rocket reveal, new satellite service available
- Appreciation – Sponsor appreciation banquet, employee awards picnic
- Celebration – Holiday gala, planet conjunction function, Moon landing, a new rocket launch, award presentation
- Conference or expo- Aerospace Day, SpaceCom, Space Symposium
- Competition – STEM robotic competition, wing/rocket/engineering design challenge

Online or virtual events proved to be very popular and a valuable tool. Its usefulness became a lifeline for many event-goers as COVID reared its ugly head. The COVID lockdown provided an opportunity for many people to attend virtually. In addition, it provided a new opportunity for some potential attendees who would not normally be able to attend the in-person version.

Ticket costs, available leave time, and travel expenses make it difficult for a large portion of the populous to get the experience or exposure of countless conferences. Many of the hosts were surprised at record turnouts for their virtual events. This makes hybrid conferences a major consideration for the future. I, for one, hope that this trend continues as the world opens up.

The benefits of events include the opportunity for engagement with a brand's audience, vendors, suppliers, colleagues, and people of influence. It is an occasion for the tribe to come together.

Invitations for speakers, dignitaries, experts, and officials increase stature, enhances influence, expands brand awareness, and create opportunities for interaction.

Benefits to events:

Here are a few of the potential benefits of creating an event.

- Builds brand awareness
- Establishes industry expertise
- Provides a story for content
- Expands network opportunities
- Provides opportunities for goodwill
- Promotes the industry (strong industry = more opportunities)
- Ignites imagination
- Provides a future pipeline for employees
- Enhances social credibility

CONFERENCES

This type of event goes by several different names such as conference, expo, summit, convention, and congress. They provide a wealth of opportunities to be heard, seen, and interact with individuals within that particular industry.

Hosting, sponsoring, vendoring, and speaking at these events help build brand awareness and can establish you, your company, or your brand as the industry expert. It puts your brand in front of a specific audience that deeply cares about the focus of the event.

Hosting the event can be a powerful opportunity for a brand. When you host, it arranges your brand to be the contact that reaches out to key players in the industry to sponsor, vendor, speak, and attend such a gathering. It places the host company in a special place as the leader.

The first conference does not have to be a large affair. It may take a few times to get the recipe right and figure out what works.

Select interesting subjects with good speakers. You want attendees to be excited that they came and return home filled with inspiration. The audience's attendance will influence actions and spread information which will grow the space industry.

A good experience at the show will bring the crowd back to the next event. It is recommended to conduct dry runs with the speakers to avoid any technical issues before their session begins.

Focus on delivering a quality event that provides a win-win-win experience for all involved and it will build into the future.

SPONSORSHIP

Events can be small and local or huge and international. Each one builds momentum and can provide a positive impact for all involved. The beautiful thing is that you do not have to do it solo. There are other companies that are looking to partner for positive exposure. Sponsorships can be designed for different levels, each one with a different benefit structure.

Likewise, sponsoring an event can provide loads of return for brand awareness and credibility. Different sponsorship levels usually offer different levels of exposure. The more exposure, the higher the cost. The right event can give your brand a lot of bang for the buck and can position your company as a leader within the industry. Choose events that cater to your audience.

If your brand decides to host an event, establish win-win situations when you build your event's sponsorship levels and event sponsorship opportunities. Create occasions to provide exposure to those sponsors who support the event the most. This does not have to add huge costs to the event's overhead. Many sponsors or partners will help build the tools that need to be created to make your event shine.

Most sponsors and partners want the exposure of their brand and are happy to pay for the chance to be included. Advertising has changed over the past decade, and it is difficult for a brand to be heard among the crowd. Sponsorship provides a vehicle to get their name in front of their audience. It is a high value in today's market.

I helped create and manage the sponsor program for a classic car cruise for 12 years. My business partner and I began the sponsorship program by adjusting the levels, creating opportunities for sponsor exposure, and establishing appreciation events to honor the sponsors. We were able to get special events paid and increase the total sponsorship tally by 700%.

This sponsorship strategy helped to bring in special guests and speakers with our sponsors' support that enhanced the event and brought larger crowds. Sponsors at a certain level had the opportunity to sponsor the speaker or guest. They paid for all of the costs associated with that speaker. In turn, their name was prominent with that key event. The event was better for it, the sponsors got exposure with enhanced social creds, the speaker expanded their fan base, and the audience enjoyed the show. Everyone won!

We utilized what we had for sponsor level creation. We gave them prominent locations on the event website, ad spots in the program, marketing materials giveaways, signage, speaking opportunities, and additional opportunities to provide the value sponsors sought while creating the sponsor levels we needed to cover costs.

When crafting the sponsorship levels, it is important to provide incentives that encourage sponsors to advance to the next level. Don't give away prominent spots to every level.

For example, the lowest level can be in a text listing on a web page, the next level adds a link to the listing, then the next level adds a logo with the link. The top levels are featured on the home page of the site. The tippy-top level should be reserved for the honorable spot with the name of the event such as Event Name - Sponsored by *Rockets-R-Us* or *Rockets-R-Us'* sponsors Event Name. This top spot would have the sponsor's name as part of the event's logo and would be added every time the event name is spoken.

Many of the sponsors were willing to help pay an extra cost to have ad space in the event program or cover the cost of a special promotion. The opportunity to purchase an ad was unlocked at a certain level providing an incentive to increase their sponsorship. The extra funds help cover the cost of the design and printing of the program or promotion.

This is a powerful strategy that benefits all of the parties involved if done correctly. It is a delicate balance to grow the event, provide tools that make happy sponsors, and provide a quality experience for your audience. It can be considered a success if everyone wants to do it again next year.

BRAND PARTNERSHIPS

Brand partnerships are a great way to magnify marketing efforts. Note: A brand partnership is different from a business partnership. A brand partnership refers to a mutual agreement to help each other to increase brand exposure, break into new markets, add extra capital, provide a specialized service, and add credibility to each other's activities, products, or services. It can add a buzz in the news while providing stories for additional content.

An example of brand partnering can be seen with Virgin Galactic. They partnered with Under Armour to produce the next generation of spacewear with their Limited Capsule Collection for the future space tourists.

They also partnered with Land Rover and Trek bicycles. Their audience is consistent with the brand partners' audiences while the revenue received from the partnership helped continue to build Virgin Galactic's expensive spaceships.

COMPETITIONS

Competitions are a great way to generate awareness for your company. All sides of the event can create a buzz about it. The host of the event, the competing participants, the sponsors, and the fans all have a part to play in this strategy.

Create a competition

Creating a competition is a great way to get attention. It can benefit all of the entities and audiences involved while stirring excitement. It is considered newsworthy and can generate articles in publications or interviews on television or podcasts.

Benefits

The organizer that creates the competition wins in several areas. A competition provides a platform for several income streams. Sponsorships, naming rights, vendors, and event competitors can help pay for the event with entry fees, ticket sales, and memorabilia sales. The surrounding area businesses benefit from the event and in turn, most of them will support it and get involved.

Everyone helps promote a competition. A competition or event will maximize the organizer's outreach (or marketing) efforts. Sponsors will promote it because it promotes themselves and makes them look good. Competitors promote it because it is an interest to them and their tribe. It makes them feel special and in-the-know.

The competition provides a platform for the organizer's cause to be heard. This event grows their audience who support their message. A competition fuels the future with donors and volunteers.

It generates excitement about the subject of the competition whether it be drone races or renewable energy. If you are going to begin a competition, make sure that it aligns with your brand, so you get the most out of it.

A great space example of a global competition is the XPRIZE. The XPRIZE Foundation began in 1994. They created seventeen competitions in the areas of Space, Oceans, Learning, Health,

Energy, Environment, Transportation, Safety, and Robotics. These competitions are designed to initiate industry breakthroughs in technology that benefits the planet.

The first Ansari XPRIZE offered $10 million for private spaceflight. This sparked a new industry and created major breakthroughs in spaceflight. On October 4, 2004, Ansari XPRIZE captured the world's attention by awarding the largest XPRIZE of $10 million to Mojave Aerospace Ventures (soon to be known as Virgin Galactic) for their SpaceShipOne.

The attention wasn't just about the large prize amount. It was also about the industry that won the prize. Up until this moment, space flight was the exclusive purview of government. Space exploration for the private sector was not possible due to regulations nor was it an affordable endeavor. Up until this point, space tourism was considered too dangerous and too expensive for the general public.

The $10 million Ansari XPRIZE, named for the multimillion-dollar donors Anousheh and Amir Ansari, was created to provide incentives for the first non-government organization to launch a reusable crewed spacecraft twice into space within a two-week period. This event was designed to lower the risk and cost for creators to make a reliable, reusable, privately financed, crewed spaceship that would place private space travel into the commercial arena. This event launched a new $2 billion private space industry.

A competition does not have to be a global affair in order to make an impact. It could be a Governor proclaimed Aerospace Day that brings a state's industry together for a one-day event that has a Wing Design Challenge for high school students, a drone race for teens, or a robotics competition for the community.

Competitions impact industries with game-changing technology. It promotes ideas, communities, industries, and companies. It labels the associated brands with ideals that are worthy endeavors. This creates fans and loyalty because it supports causes that people find important.

Be in a competition

Participating in a competition has many benefits. It is a way to prove your company's capabilities and provide a reason to expand or polish them. It exposes your competencies to a new audience and provides a reason for more content.

The XPRIZE competition launched a $2 billion private space industry that made private space travel a viable commercial enterprise thus encouraging many new technological advances.

In the previous example, the Mojave Aerospace Ventures team won the first $10 million XPRIZE then licensed the winning technology to Richard Branson. He then created Virgin Galactic.

Winning the XPRIZE provided valuable exposure for the baby company of Virgin Galactic. It provided a platform to introduce the company to the space industry as well as the public. Winning the competition established them as the expert in space tourism.

Big or small, a competition can provide a win for all.

Naming rights

Since the first XPRIZE, there have been several new XPRIZE competitions added to the offerings. XPRIZE has provided naming rights for large donations towards a particular competition. With over $140 million in prizes, companies and individuals have partners with XPRIZE just to be associated with such campaigns as the $10 million Qualcomm Tricorder XPRIZE and the $1.4 million Wendy Schmidt Oil Cleanup XPRIZE.

Google has jumped at the XPRIZE sponsorship with the Google Lunar XPRIZE. It is a competition focused on privately funded lunar exploration. The largest of several awards is $20 million to be awarded to the first privately funded team to produce a robot that lands on the Moon and travels 500m (1,640 ft) across its surface.

The Google Lunar XPRIZE launched in 2007. It hoped to accomplish several things: Create affordable access to the moon; provide a platform for long-term entrepreneurial development focused on lunar transportation; and inspire the next generation of scientists, engineers, and space explorers.

User-generated content

Including user-generated content helps a brand create new, meaningful content and provides an opportunity for relevant recognition of participants of the competition. Employing user-generated content (UGC) strategies can expand the conversation, connect with your brand's audience, and generate excitement for the competition.

Content from these competitions and/or contests could include videos from the contestants, news footage from the event, or stories highlighting the participants on the website. Add ways where the contestants can share their content. Provide ready-to-use content and tools that can be individualized and makes their participation easy to share on their social platforms.

APPLY IT

Your brand does not have to start from scratch. There are entities that offer ready-to-go STEM competitions like MindCraft, Virgin Galactic, and NASA. NASA has created a comprehensive list of competitions design to build interest in careers ranging from robotics to aviation.

Even a small competition can produce events that pull in leadership from local governments that can create opportunities for goodwill with them and the community. Processes do not have to be significant to reap rewards in time.

Look at NASA's website
https://www.nasa.gov/aeroresearch/resources/design-competitions

CHAPTER 17

EDUCATION-BASED STRATEGY

William Penn: "Knowledge is the treasure of a wise man"
Nelson Mandela: "Education is the most powerful weapon to change the world."

One of your brand's most valuable asset is your industry expertise. Using this expertise to help your audience solve their problems sets up the company to be a trusted resource for information within the industry. In its truest form, education-based marketing uses knowledge to empower an audience and gain their trust. This type of strategy spreads ideas and builds industries.

Build trust

Many businesses see their audience as sheep-to-shear. This one-way relationship does not work well as consumers have more power in what they see, hear, and experience. Smart businesses help their audience grow and give them the tools they need to make an educated decision about their activities.

Educational-based marketing is a strategy that contributes value and earns an audience's trust and loyalty. The content should be created with the goal of fulfilling our audience's needs and interests. Audiences are more receptive to educational messages that offer information and facts that help them fill their knowledge void, get past their pain points, and aids in their decision-making.

Educational-based strategy can build a stronger relationship between you and your audience.

As your brand gives advice and knowledge, this strategy works when there is not a requirement of anything in return. It establishes your brand as the expert and a reliable source of information. When it comes time to purchase, your brand will be top-of-mind and a rapport will already be established.

Build content

As you develop content, keep in mind that people don't care about your brand's products or services; they care about their problems and seek solutions. Using an education strategy gives a reason to develop conversations through content. As your audience consumes the answers to their problems, they will also learn about the industry and your company's services, products, and activities.

If your brand is considered the expert and your audience seek out the information, it must be provided without any strings attached. Your audience will accept that the information is legitimate and isn't a sales pitch if it is freely given. Don't try to trick them into a sales pitch along this journey. If you break this trust, they will never come back.

When it is time to buy, they will be more likely to go with the entity that they have begun to trust. They will not go with the companies that shouted ads at them, but with the company that invested its effort into making the customer better and smarter.

Your educational approach should be that of providing pure value and expecting nothing in return.

As Chet Holmes puts it… *"When you try to sell, you break rapport. No one wants to be "sold." But when you "educate," you BUILD rapport. You build respect, trust, influence, all key ingredients to making a sale."*

Educational content

One of the best ways to decide what topics should be in your educational strategy is to look at the questions your audience are already asking. We discussed this task in the audience section. Ask them through surveys and interviews with open-ended questions. You may discover roadblocks or new opportunities by spending time with your potential and current customers.

Educational strategies work because the company demonstrates an investment in helping its audience. It works because it makes the audience feel like they are part of the team and they become invested in the outcome.

NASA is a great example of an organization that uses this educational marketing strategy. NASA uses this technique to build the idea of space, fill the pipeline with stargazed professionals, and shape an industry. They share their knowledge with the public and are dedicated to making it accessible and digestible.

NASA began building the Apollo program using the education marketing model. NASA was focused on educating the public. It worked with thousands of partners to multiply its efforts to get as much educational content out into the public awareness as possible. It produced television reels that would demonstrate how rockets worked, hands-on models that traveled the country, thick manuals for the media about everything they would need to know in order to produce the news, and so much more.

NASA states: *"Education is an essential part of NASA's mission to drive advances in science, technology, aeronautics, and space exploration to enhance knowledge, education, innovation, economic vitality, and stewardship of Earth."*

NASA sees how this strategy benefits them in the long-term. They focus on developing quality multi-touchpoint educational content that informs and inspires on as many channels as possible.

When writing this book, NASA had 1,614 results on their website for STEM Resources and Opportunities. That is dedication. Their focus is *"Inspire – engage – educate - employ."*

NASA provides content through every step of the journey. Imagine a bright-eyed child watching a NASA video about how a rocket gets made. They are inspired and build one of the rockets in the STEM courses that NASA offers on their website. They are intrigued and research more about fuels through NASA's huge library of articles, publications, and videos. That curiosity stays with that child, and they grow up to be an engineer. They go to work for NASA after college. NASA invested its efforts into building that child's dream. In response, that child invested their lives into a shared dream with NASA. That connects them in a powerful way.

No one has come close to building a brand with the results that NASA has accomplished. NASA's educational marketing efforts are probably the reason you are dedicated to space. I know it is for me.

If you have only one case study for marketing, NASA is a great example.

APPLY IT:

Gather information from current customers and potential customers to determine what kind of information and education they need. It is important to talk to them to gather this information. (I know... I am a broken record)

There are several tools that can be used for gathering this information. Interviews will work best for gathering this type of information. It is surprising what you will learn. During this process, you can learn about roadblocks and opportunities that you didn't know existed. Make sure you use unbiased and open-ended questions that will spark a free-flowing answer. Make sure that you let the participant talk and don't impede them until you are sure they have finished answering the question.

What problems do your customers experience?
Retrace their steps along the journey to the very beginning of their discovery. How can you provide education earlier in your customer's journey?

Let's use our fictitious example. *Rockets-R-Us* is looking to build educational content for its audience. Questions they may ask are:
- What problems do satellites solve?
- What are other solutions that can be used instead of satellites?
- What criteria do target companies use to decide to use a satellite to solve their problem?
- What information did they look for when they began their research?
- What tools do target companies need to plan/make a satellite?
- What are some pitfalls that can happen when building a satellite?
- What do the target companies need to know when planning/making/launching a satellite?

- What criteria do the target companies use in deciding a launch option?

Companies are starting to provide bundling services as a result of some of these answers. A book that I recommend reading about providing answers is *They Ask, You Answer* by Marcus Sheridan. He demonstrates the value of education and how it saved his swimming pool business.

Educational marketing is one of the most powerful marketing strategies out there. The research into deciding what content to use brings you closer to your audience. It pulls people to your brand and establishes trust. It is marketing that feels more like friendship.

PART 3

WHAT'S NEXT

So, you made it this far. You probably want to know how to make these marketing strategies happen.

The key to a successful marketing program is to establish a culture that places importance on the discipline. A successful culture begins with leadership. If they/you are not on board, marketing initiatives will fizzle.

CHAPTER 18

BUDGET

GETTING CREATIVE

I love the idea of keeping things scrappy. I think having a tight budget can make us more innovative. This scrappiness only works when the goal is about achieving the most **IMPACT** with our resources and finite energies. These steps can work with any project that is being considered, including marketing strategies.

Step 1: What's the goal?

Like a map, you need to know where you are going before you can plot a course on the map. These goals need to be clear and have complete buy-in from those involved. Determine the goal of the project before continuing to the next step.

Step 2: What is needed to accomplish the goal?

Think really BIG, and act like there are not any limits to the available funding and no hurdles to overcome in order to accomplish the goal. The world is perfect and think like there is an abundance of money. What would your team create to meet this challenge?

This step must be done first and without the constraints of costs or obstacles. Use your imagination and let the brainstorming explode.

Step 3: Ask "How can we achieve the same result with little or no money?"

This will get the creative juices flowing without jeopardizing or constraining the grand idea in Step 2. If you jump to this step first, it will limit the unseen opportunities and restrict your vision to a lower level of possibility. Dream first, then let reality come into the mix. So, we have this big, audacious idea, how can it be done with our current resources? By asking "how," the mind begins to solve the problem. The result is a creative option that may be better than the dream.

Step 4: Ask "Can we share the costs with a partner, vendor, or other entity?"

Someone else may be willing and eager to share the opportunity. A strategic partner can expand your projects' reach and audience as well as share the costs. Make sure that they complement your brand, and that the roles and responsibilities are very clear before beginning the venture. Remember *that you are who you hang around* so, don't enter into any agreement with a company that will harm your brand's reputation just to offset any costs.

Step 5: Ask "Now, can we earn income with this idea?"

Some marketing strategies can be shifted around to generate an income. How great is that?! Sponsorships, partnerships, affiliates, ticketing, and other opportunities can be alluring to other companies that share your same target audience. They may be willing to pay for the privilege of sharing them.

CAUTION: Be cautious when charging your audience and make sure that it adds to the perceived value. Perceived value is what the "thing" is worth in the eyes of the receiver. There are many things that are accessible in this modern-day and your brand's audience may not be willing to pay for this access. In fact, it may be offensive and serve as a friction point that turns them away.

On the flip side, free is not always a good thing. Free can mean that it is NOT worth having, there may be strings tied to it, or it's a trick. Your audience may be expecting or willing to pay to be a part of the event or idea. When there is an investment, it generates respect for the value of "it" and creates the feeling of being part of an exclusive club.

Trend carefully when charging your audience. Make sure that it is a part of the strategy and not a fleecing. Fleecing will destroy relationships that your brand may *never* be able to repair.

Income versus cost

Marketing that earns income can be more effective than marketing that costs money. What?! Yes, that's right.! It is a beautiful thing.

Many tactics from traditional marketing efforts are seen as invasive and are increasingly blocked as audiences acquire the technology to avoid ads and other forms of paid advertising. I could write several books on this subject, but there is already a really good one available. This point is preached by a marketer of one of my favorite books. Let me introduce you to Joe Pulizzi and his book, *Killing Marketing*. His book has good tips about marketing strategies that are useful, but he teaches a different way of thinking about how marketing is done. He has interesting case studies that can change the perception of what marketing can be, and illustrates income-producing marketing strategies that are can be more effective than their budget-draining counterparts.

There are many opportunities for marketing initiatives to provide an income from t-shirt sales to promotional partnerships. How many of you own NASA t-shirts, mugs, or blankets? Have you monetized your YouTube channel? Sold any tickets into orbit?

CHAPTER 19

HIRE TALENT

Marketing is a profession that embodies education and expertise just as other critical positions. Experience is important if you want your marketing program to work. You can't hire your cousin's kid who is taking a marketing class in college and expect it to make major positive impacts in the brand. In fact, poor marketing can have negative impacts on your brand.

Unless you love marketing more than building space stuff, you will need to find someone who does love marketing. Marketing is a discipline that is just as focused as an engineer. Look to bring talent on board.

Talent is important in any position. Marketing is not any different. Would you have your accountant building a rocket instead of an engineer? Then don't assign marketing as a side gig for one of your staff, including your sales reps.

Marketing IS about selling but it is NOT the same as sales. Marketing is a bullhorn for the brand and sales is the human contact. Sales is a facet of marketing.

Marketing is the introduction of the brand to your audience. It sets the tone and builds trust. It provides the creative direction for campaigns, creates materials, and develops content that represents the brand. It embodies the customer experience and engages with the brand's audiences. Marketing makes the company brand look competent and attractive. It educates audiences and answers questions.

Marketing is ALL of the branding activities that bring the customer to the sales reps. It provides the sales reps with the tools that they need to enhance the customer's journey. Marketing creates branding activities that grab attention and bring the customers back for more.

Marketing establishes the brand personality and gets the attention of the audience. Sales is the human interaction.

Sometimes these two positions get lumped into one. To make matters more confusing, many sales jobs have marketing in the title because the employer wants it to sound better. Sales reps should be allowed the time to do their jobs to the best of their abilities. It takes a different set of skills to close the sale and work with the customer. They cannot do an effective job if they are running off to shoot a video or writing an article.

Historically, marketing and sales have been different departments and have operated in silos. I don't think this is effective either. Sales is an important facet of the marketing process. The sales team dedicate their efforts to make sure that the customer's experience is fulfilling and positive. To do this effectively, the sales team need to be supported and their needs heard by the marketing team. In turn, the marketing efforts need to influence how sales is conducted. They cannot be effective if they are exclusive. They need to have a symbiotic relationship in order to make it work.

The marketing team need to create campaigns and maintain branding. This includes:
- creating content (videos, articles, post campaigns, etc.)
- monitor activity and analytics
- create presentations
- run social platforms
- expand the website
- attend events
- serve as a guest speaker on podcasts or at conferences
- establish a public affairs program

- conduct educational outreach
- and so much more.

The sales team need to focus on helping the customer and making sure their needs are met. These positions and responsibilities are very different.

When it comes to implementing marketing initiatives, there are two choices for hiring talent. You can hire an agency, or you can hire someone in-house to add to your team.

It is important to have a person(s) in place whose only focus is to promote the company. There are a lot of moving parts in today's online world including search engines, social media, podcasts, video, television, and websites. It needs to be an important component for the overall business activities. Having the right person can build brand awareness, bring opportunities, and generate income for the company.

INTERNAL VS EXTERNAL
HIRE AN AGENCY
PRO:

• Agencies have a team of creative professionals that focus on their individual disciplines, such as videographer, graphics, writers, etc. This allows your company to plug into that expertise when you need it without having to staff it.

• If they do not have the needed expertise within the agency staff, they have a network of freelancers that can accomplish the targeted creative need.

• Agencies have expertise within their focused markets. Each agency has a specialized niche that they know the current trends and outlets within their industry. You will want to get an agency that has experience within your industry. For example, an agency that focuses on automobiles may not be able to accommodate the same level of expertise for launching a new breakfast cereal.

• Agencies have connections within their niche industry. In the example above, the agency may have connections with a car magazine and can provide an article that becomes a feature story. Unfortunately, that is useless if you are a cereal company that needs to get into grocery stores.

CONS:

• **Expensive**
It can be expensive to hire an agency to handle your marketing needs. Budgets may restrict hiring an agency.

• **Lack of space industry-focused agencies.**
As of this writing, there were only a few agencies that focused on the space industry. This will change as the industry expands.

• Creative limitations

Agencies can only work with what you give them. They can be the most talented agency in the world, but they can only see your company through the lens of their point of contact within your company and what they can gather from the content already existing in the public domain. This can constrain creative opportunities because the agency becomes limited by what the company *chooses* to give them.

We tend to become desensitized by the everyday flow. What may seem ordinary and unremarkable could be something quite special to your audience. Many opportunities for engagement with an audience are lost because those immersed in the day-to-day don't see it.

The opposite can be true. Materials given by an inventor or engineer may seem interesting to them but could fall flat because it is too complicated or is missing context.

• Limited time

When there is not a dedicated marketing person and things are busy, it can be difficult to find the time to gather the information that the agencies need to develop a new piece of content. Content that is in development can grow stale because it is waiting for an edit, review, or a signoff.

What to look for in hiring an agency:

Prior work

Look at their prior work. Does it demonstrate quality and the style that you want to be reflected in your brand? Do they have similar clients? Do they have experience with your brand's type of audience? Are they familiar with the channels your audience uses, and do they have the necessary experience to produce content on those channels?

All of these questions should be considered when choosing the agency that will represent your brand.

Talk to their clients

It is always a good idea to talk to people who have worked with the agency before. Were they easy to works with? Did they return calls in a timely manner? Did they provide clear plans for projects? Did they meet deadlines? Did their campaign ideas work?

Make sure that you can use the assets

Copyrights are assigned to the creator/agency even if you paid them to do it unless it is stipulated in the contract. Many agencies require their created content to be used exclusively through them. There are several reasons for this arrangement. It prompts more financial interactions, makes it harder to be replaced by another agency, and provides the agency with creative control which safeguards their reputation.

You can negotiate different terms that include the copyright, but it will cost a lot more. Expect to pay double, triple, or more for complete copyrights to the creative files. If you do not have complete copyright for any layout or artwork, you will be held liable if you use, or have anyone else use, the files or duplicate them. Think of it as someone using your patent and duplicating your invention.

The agency's assets can include *your* website domains and *your* hosting. **If you ask the agency to get a domain and they purchase it, it is *their* asset, not *yours*.** I highly recommend establishing your own domain in your own hosting account and give the agency access to it. If they own the website hosting account where your website is parked and there is a fallout, all of your website content could be deleted or locked. It could get very ugly and costly to replace your domain.

HIRE PROFESSIONALS FOR YOUR IN-HOUSE TEAM

Starting out

Even if you opt for the agency route, you will need to have someone on staff that makes marketing a priority. Someone will need to work with the agency and be the point person for marketing initiatives. They will need to be knowledgeable about the marketing needs of the company and the process.

PROS:

• Participation in company's daily activities

Agencies do not have an intimate knowledge of the day-to-day operations of your business. By having permanent staff, they can capitalize on opportunities to develop stories and content about things that happen every day. These are things that only a staff member will see and be able to quickly utilize.

• One vision

The in-house staffing provides a cohesive vision that is brand-forward. They can focus on developing the brand with campaigns and content.

• Complete focus and dedication

In-house staff has 100% focus on the company's brand. Agencies work with other clients. If it is a niche agency, some clients could be competitors. Content that was developed for your company could be recycled for another company. Other companies can bump your projects if they have a more intense deadline, or they are deemed to be more profitable.

• Be a point of contact

An in-house staff member can be the point person for the times when you may want to access an agency or freelance talent for a particular project. A marketing staff member should know who to go to, what to ask for, handle contracts and budgeting, handle the editing process, be able to determine the quality of the delivered asset, determine where/how it should be used, and make sure that the delivered asset fits with the company's brand.

• Company owns assets

When you hire a marketing person to be on staff, it should be stipulated in the contract that all assets that were created by the employee during the hours that they are paid belong to the company.

CONS:

• Constant cost

A staff member has a salary. An agency can be hired as-needed. As with any employee, you have employer benefits, taxes, and fees that can cost more than their salary depending. Employee benefits add on to the final cost.

Limited skills

If you hire one person, they could be gifted in many different skills. However, there will be some aspects that they may be weaker in than others. Even the most gifted people will have to offset some skills. In contrast, agencies have a pool of videographers, designers, and writers that are specialized in particular skill sets.

Note: You may not need award-winning videos if phone-captured video clips connect better with your audience. Don't sacrifice 100 touches of fun video posts with your audience in exchange for one excellent video that comes off too polished. Sometimes it is the phone-captured moments that feel more authentic and connect better.

Valuable assets

The aspects below are based on assumptions that you have not hired a person for your team yet and are looking to hire your first marketing professional.

Leadership

You will want someone that can lead a team as the marketing department demonstrates success and grows. This skill is important for dealing with agencies, media, and even the company itself. You want someone that knows when to fight for a project and when to let one go.

Balanced skillset

You should look for a balanced skillset. If you can find someone who can create captivating campaigns, is a technician that can create graphics and video, AND is a leader, then snatch them up right away! More than likely, you will find someone with a range of strengths.

Creative ideas

Creativity is the most important quality. Technical abilities can be augmented with available tools or outsourced using freelance talent. It is more important to high someone with creative ideas for campaigns that work.

Is it more important to have someone who can create an idea for a new rocket engine versus someone who just turns a wrench?

Easy to work with

A good marketing person will need to work with many different people from many different disciplines. Aim for a person that can engage in conversation and can pull insights from all of the different people within your company and from your audience. The insights that can be gathered are important to developing engaging content.

A talented person with a great attitude can be taught the nuts and bolts of the organization. On the flip side, it may be harder to teach someone that is a subject matter expert how to be engaging.

Monetization

This is a new one for many businesses in the field. Technology advances have provided many opportunities for marketing strategies to provide income. Many of these tactics actually work better than traditional strategies that drain the budget. I recommend this particular skill be present in your staff member... if you can find it. Keep in mind that this is not a common skill.

Content development

A good marketing person will understand branding, content development, monetization, layout (graphics and video), and monetized marketing efforts that can provide new income streams.

If you are a small company looking for an initial person that can grow the company and the marketing department, you will want someone with a breadth of skills.
- Can they great engaging content experiences?
- Can they design and manage a website?

- Do they know how to build relational campaigns with an audience?
- Can they write content?
- Are they able to create engaging images?
- Are they good at presentations?
- Can they turn marketing initiatives into income-producing opportunities?

PHILOSOPHY CHANGE

There are many new ways to market a company. Many of these new tactics cost nothing but the payroll of your staff. Some of these tactics can even generate income and they can be more effective than paid advertising. If you can find this quality in your employee, they are worth their weight in gold.

It is important to understand that a marketing professional has invested their career in the study of human behavior. This quality will impact all aspects of your company from establishing the perception of the company within the industry to customer experiences. In addition, they can influence talent acquisition and employee satisfaction. Marketing impacts how people see the organization.

SMALL MARKETING TEAM

Once your company dives into marketing, you will find that it requires a certain number of skills to do this journey correctly. Eventually, you may opt to grow your team. There are several members that you will want to add. These include a videographer, a graphic designer, a journalist, a social media maven, and a website guru. Some people may have a combination of these skills allowing for fewer people. It is a balance of budget versus need as you increase in size.

Each of these positions requires focus and dedication to do them correctly. If your videographer can spend the week making videos, they will produce more content than someone who can only spend one day per week on the effort.

This team can expand or shrink depending on your needs. Just like working on a rocket, how many skilled people are on the team affects how much can get accomplished and the speed at which it happens.

Roles

The roles listed below are the roles that will make a strong small team. Some of the skills may be present within different roles such as analytic skills. The roles can reside in fewer people or be added to your company as marketing needs grow. Some of these roles can be outsourced through agencies or freelance talent until they are hired into the team. These are listed in order of priority of importance.

Marketing leadership:

A leader will need to be a hub and responsible for the marketing initiatives and content that the company releases into the world. You will need a person that can lead a team, keep everyone on brand, and keep projects on schedule. This person should have the creative vision for strategic marketing campaigns and the ability to lead their team to accomplish them. They should understand how to motivate creative thinkers and stimulate ideas.

Journalist/writer:

There is power in words. They are vital for search engines and promotions. You will need someone that knows how to write. This person should be skilled at storytelling and can create prose that is engaging. This personality needs to work well with other departments and be skilled at gathering information through interviews and editing contributions from coworkers. Writing needs can include press releases, articles, web content, social media content, training, and manuals.

This is an important member of the team. They will need to work with subject matter experts within the company and coax important information from them. They need to be able to take gathered information and transform it into an engaging piece of prose.

Website guru:

Your website is where your digital assets reside. A website person should understand the user's experience and understand how to maximize it. They need technical skills to build and maintain a website and understand the programming involved. In addition, they need to know SEO strategies and analytics. There is a wide range of abilities. Abilities range from basic website proficiency to managing dynamic sites that employ things such as gaming or virtual reality.

The digital environment is constantly evolving. The top skills recommended for this person are the drive to be a lifelong learner and the dedication to the user experience. Programs and skills can be added, but not attitude.

Graphic designer:

A graphic designer creates and edits images for articles, website, social media, and video. Prepares educational and sales materials, signage, and giveaway items. Many of these graphics need to be prepped for different formats. Other duties may include photography.

The top skill in this position is the ability to tell a story through a visual medium.

Social media maven:

Conversations are everywhere. Social content has rules, and each platform has individual needs to maximize their power. This person needs to know how to navigate social media platforms, setup a social calendar, post and schedule content, monitor and reply to comments, monitor conversations of the industry and competitors, and analyze the analytics.

The top skill in this position is the ability to represent the brand, its message, and its personality. This person embodies the voice and can minimize or eliminate tricky issues that arise from social conversations. In other words, you do NOT want a hothead in this position. Internet conversation can take on a life of its own and erupt in ways that you would never expect.

Videographer:

This person makes videos that can be used for information, promotion, entertainment, education, and training. These will include bite-sized clips for social media, a longer format for YouTube, and substantial lengths for training and education. Videographers spend their time planning videos, scripting, capturing video, trimming and organizing clips, adding effects, editing, finding music and sound effects, finalizing, posting, and online prep. Other duties may include photography.

Top skill for this position is the ability to tell a story that is engaging and brand-forward.

Code of Ethics

Each member needs to understand and adhere to a specific code of ethics. These are the ethics that I adhere to in my work.

- Practice the core values of honesty, integrity, excellence, and respect.

- Be responsible for what you create.

- Recognize any facts that may jeopardize the integrity of a story or content.

- Minimize potential harm to sources or subjects of stories.

- Always credit sources of content or ideas. If a person created it, then they own the copyright to it. Never plagiarize or repurpose someone else's written words, images, photos, or other media without permission.

- Be sure the audience understands the intent of the content.

- Do not deceive or lie. Ever.

- Disclose all potential conflicts of interest or any appearance of conflict.

Marketing is a powerful discipline that can put a man on the Moon and bring positive changes to our world. It is powerful enough to create peace or start a war. Make sure that you and your team are ethical in its use.

CONCLUSION

Space – the ~~final~~ NEXT frontier.

There have been major leaps in the space industry in the past two decades. Even with COVID, the space industry shows amazing potential as the next decade begins.

Events that marked 2020:

- SpaceX and NASA launched astronauts to the ISS.
- China's Chang'e 5 landed on the Moon and returned a sample to Earth. (first country since 1976)
- Japan's Hayabusa2 returned asteroid samples to Earth.
- Christina Koch sets a record for 328 days of continuous time aboard the ISS by a woman.

The first half of 2021 was an amazing year in space.

- Space tourism took off where Sir Branson and Jeff Bezos flew on their first official tourism flights.
- Perseverance and Ingenuity demonstrated many firsts with sight, sound and flight on Mars. China achieved Mars orbit and Tianwen-1 rover lands on Mars.
- Emirates Mars Mission Hope orbiter reaches Mars.
- China launched their first space station module.
- SpaceX's Starship landed successfully.
- OSIRIS-REx to begin its voyage home with an asteroid sample from Bennu.

Many more events are set to happen in the second half of 2021 including:

- NASA's launches Artemis-1 Moon mission.
- Starship spacecraft to conduct an orbital test flight.
- Blue Origin's New Glenn rocket slated to reach orbit.
- Boeing's Starliner space capsule anticipated to make its first crewed flight to the International Space Station.

- Peregrine lunar lander will ride aboard its United Space Alliance's Vulcan Centaur first flight.
- James Webb Space Telescope is set to launch.
- First commercial lander touch to down on the moon.
- NASA is set to launch the Lucy spacecraft that will visit Trojan asteroids that share an orbit with Jupiter.

...and so much more.

Space is evolving at an unprecedented rate. More than 70 countries have embarked on space-related aspirations that will change our Earthy landscape. New opportunities and increased competition will require the business model to change for space-focused companies.

Marketing and brand development will become more important than ever as the industry expands. Marketing activities set your company apart from its growing competition. This could be the deciding factor in acquiring a grant, contract, or customers.

Space Marketing is the first book in a series. In future books, I will take a deeper look into specific space sectors and their marketing opportunities, challenges and straggles. These space sectors will include spaceports, the Moon, Mars, the ISS, and LEO space.

I love space and want to help the industry continue to grow. Developing space activities will impact new technologies that will make Earth cleaner, improve lives, and increase our knowledge of the universe. It is so much more than just seeking the stars.

I hope that you found this book useful and that some of these tips and principles will help your company grow.

I am excited to see what you do with space.

Thank you!

If you have enjoyed this book and found it to be of value, please leave a review.

Sign up for information about new book launches on my website at https://izzy.house.

A list of references for this book are available on my website at https://izzy.house/space-marketing-book/

Made in the USA
Monee, IL
15 October 2021